Hidden in The Garden

(God's Hidden Mysteries from the Garden of Eden...Revealed)

Jer 33:3
3 Call unto me, and I will answer thee, and shew thee
great and mighty things, which thou knowest not.
KJV

Biblical
TEACHER
Samuel
Williams

Hidden in The Garden
(God's Hidden Mysteries from the Garden of Eden...Revealed)

Copyright © 2017 by Samuel Williams
All rights reserved.
ISBN-13: 978-1978325739
ISBN-10: 1978325738
Samuel Williams

To order additional copies, visit
www.createspace.com/7696140
Facebook page: Hidden in The Garden
http://samuelkem.wixsite.com/truthaboutthetithe
contact the author via email at samuelkem@aol.com.

Printed by Createspace an Amazon company
Printed in the United States of America 2017
First Edition

Acknowledgements

When we meet God, it will be on His terms and not ours!

I would like to dedicate this book to the woman that birthed me, gave me the name she was instructed to by God, introduced me to Christianity, saved my life on two occasions, loved me, and prayed me through this life's journey. This woman, who is still praying for me today, is my mother Carol Rose Blackwood. Thank you Ma. I truly would not be here if it were not for all the sacrifices you have made. Endless Love!

This book is also dedicated to everyone who wants a deeper understanding of the knowledge and revelations of God.

Prov 4:7
7 Wisdom is the principal thing; therefore get wisdom: and with all thy getting get understanding.
KJV

Let's Pray

Oh great and mighty God, the true and everlasting Father, God of Abraham, Isaac, and Israel. I come to You this day in the precious name of Your Son Jesus Christ of Nazareth, Yehoshua, Your Holy Arm, and Your Salvation. Father, I ask for forgiveness of sin for myself and every person that is reading this book. According to Your words, Father, that if we confess our sins that you will forgive those sins and cleanse us from all unrighteousness. Wash our feet Lord, and forgive us for the lust of the flesh, the lust of the eyes, and the pride of life. Father, I come today asking that You will anoint this book and protect the seed of Your Word that is in it. I come against the principalities, powers, rulers of the darkness of this world, and spiritual wickedness in high places. Even now, Father, they are gathering to hinder and stop the revelation of Your Word that You have placed on these pages from reaching the masses. Father, the devil is a liar. I break and rebuke every plan of the enemy in the name of Jesus (Yehoshua) and come against every plot and every blueprint that they will come to nothing. Father, I extend my covering over every one of Your children and those You are calling to salvation that gaze upon this book. Put a hedge of protection around their minds so that the enemy cannot project any thoughts of accusations or lies to stop them from reading this book. I speak peace in their minds as soon as they open these pages or pull up the eBook on their devices. I speak peace in their homes and surroundings. Your Word says they will be taught of the Lord and great will be their peace. Father, let the peace start as their eyes gaze upon the words of this book. Father, let the living waters pour out where ever they are reading so their hearts can be softened to the acceptance of Your Word. After the seed is planted Father protect the seed so the enemy cannot snatch it. I come against every distraction in the name of Jesus and every person sent to sway them away from the reading of this book. I rebuke them, in the name of Jesus. Father, open up the mysteries in Your Word unto them and increase their talents. Build them up Lord build them up. I ask all of this in the precious name of Your Son; in Jesus name I pray, to the glory and honor of the Father, amen.

Contents

Foreword

There is an old Hebrew legend that four rabbis went into the Garden of Eden (Paradise). The first rabbi dropped dead. The second rabbi went mad. The third rabbi, in disbelief, started cutting down all the plants. The last rabbi entered in and departed in peace.

The story was a warning about the allegorical nature of the beginning of Genesis to include the Garden story. Rabbis would tell this story to new students in the study of the Tanach (Jewish Bible) to warn them about the understanding and misunderstanding of Genesis. They knew the garden story contained many dark sayings (parables). God had Moses write the story in a way that would conceal the full meaning of events that took place. It is sealed, meaning the knowledge and understanding of the story is hidden. It is a mystery of the Kingdom.

I truly believe God was manifesting in me in preparation for the writing of this book before I knew Him. When I look back over my life, I can see the guiding hand of His Holy Spirit steering me into His purpose for my life. Teachers in the Body of Christ are called to teach the unbelievers the Gospel of Peace and the believers the mysteries of the Kingdom. This book contains revelations of the mysteries of the Garden of Eden. The truths, lessons, and examples in these mysteries solidify the understanding of the Word of God. They assist us in traversing the distance from faith to love and obtaining everything contained in-between. This is an expedition into the mysteries of the Garden of Eden. Please take this journey with me. Let's get started.

Matt 13:11-12
11 He answered and said unto them, because it is given unto you to know the mysteries of the kingdom of heaven, but to them it is not given.
12 For whosoever hath, to him shall be given, and he shall have more abundance: but whosoever hath not, from him shall be taken away even that he hath.
KJV (King James Version)

Introductions

The first time God spoke to me (and I knew it was Him) it came in the form of a question. He asked, "What shall I do?" I replied, "Give me knowledge and wisdom." I did not receive a response in words; I just noticed I had an overpowering urge to open up the Bible and read all night. The next night exactly the same thing happened, and the next and the next. Soon my apartment's living room floor was filled with concordances, Greek and Hebrew dictionaries, and atlas maps of Biblical lands. I was ingesting everything I could on the Bible.

Some days I would come home tired at 10:30 p.m. at night and say there would be no studying tonight. I was going to bed. The next thing I knew I was looking at the early morning sunlight streaming through the sliding glass door. I would realize that I had been studying all night. This went on for more than two years. After I received the baptism of the Holy Spirit, I started studying more than eight hours a day on most days. This type of studying went on for many years.

The day I was anointed as a teacher in the Body of Christ God spoke to me saying, "I am going to use you to bring others from where they are into My presence. You're going to be a teacher of many and they are going to know you're a man of God." God has never broken a single promise to me.

I thought this would have been the first book I would write but it ended up being my third. When you base your life on obedience to God, you have to follow His blueprint and not your own. This is the book that I wanted to write almost all my Christian life. The importance of this book is beyond measure.

Those who are capable of seeing the big picture of what is going to be revealed in these pages, you are going to spend a lot of time silently staring only to burst out with glorification of God. It has been more than 25 years since God asked me those four words, "What shall I do?" I can truly say that He did much more than I expected. What He gave me is worth, to me, more than all the riches in the world. I am going to take you on the same journey that God took me on as He walked me through the Garden of Eden. I am going to show you what God explained, clarified, and revealed. This is the mysteries of the Garden of Eden as the Holy Spirit revealed it.

Job 36:22
22 Behold, God exalteth by his power: **who teacheth like him?** KJV

Why did He reveal it to me? I have two explanations. First, He asked me what I wanted and I responded, "Knowledge and wisdom." Secondly, I believe we are so close to the end of time that the mysteries are being opened to usher in the coming of Christ Jesus (Yehoshua). How God chooses and plans peoples' lives go way beyond my pay grade. He selects people who will bring Him the glory. Therefore, He does not pick like others pick and sometimes He takes something that does not fit but then He shapes it into the perfect fit. God did this, and I am just glad He had mercy on me because I was a non-believer who spoke out against His Kingdom. The day He anointed me as a teacher in the body of Christ, I went home and with tearful eyes asked him, "Why!" After all, I had done against the Body of Christ as an unbeliever; I wanted to know why He would give me a position in Christ's Body, the church. He gave me this scripture:

1 Tim 1:12-14
12 And I thank Christ Jesus our Lord, who hath enabled me, for that **he counted me faithful, putting me into the ministry;**
13 Who was before a blasphemer, and a persecutor, and injurious: but **I obtained mercy, because I did it ignorantly in unbelief.**
14 And the grace of our Lord was exceeding abundant with faith and love which is in Christ Jesus.

Until you experience God's mercy, you have no idea what a wonderful God we serve. Father, I bless your Holy Name!

Chapter 1

It's A Coded Book

Isa 28:9-13

9 **Whom shall he teach knowledge? and whom shall he make to understand doctrine?** them that are weaned from the milk, and drawn from the breasts.

10 **For precept must be upon precept, precept upon precept; line upon line, line upon line; here a little, and there a little:**

11 For **with stammering lips and another tongue** will he speak to this people.

12 To whom he said, This is the rest wherewith ye may cause the weary to rest; and this is the refreshing: yet they would not hear.

13 But **the word of the LORD was unto them precept upon precept, precept upon precept; line upon line, line upon line; here a little, and there a little; that they might go, and fall backward, and be broken, and snared, and taken.**

KJV

You will never be able to fully understand the Bible until you realize that it is a coded book. It is not coded because I believe it to be. It is coded because the Word of God says it is coded.

Isaiah 28 above shows that those who can be taught knowledge and those who can understand doctrine are those who are no longer drinking milk. Isaiah is using the comparison of a babe drinking milk from the mother's breast as a metaphor for those too young spiritually to understand the deeper things of God.

The writer of Hebrews breaks this down and expounds on what Isaiah is trying to say by comparing the simple things of God to milk and the deep things to meat.

Heb 5:12-14
12 For when for the time ye ought to be teachers, ye have need that one teach you again which be the first principles of the oracles of God; and are become such as **have need of milk, and not of strong meat.**
13 For every one that useth milk is unskilful in the word of righteousness: for **he is a babe.**
14 But **strong meat belongeth to them that are of full age,** even those who by reason of use have their senses exercised to discern both good and evil.
KJV

Isaiah also adds that an individual has to understand that the Bible hides things that cannot be discovered until you put verses (precepts) together. Verse must be upon verse, verse upon verse. Therefore, he is literally saying you have to connect the verses together. In addition, the next line he says, "Line upon line," but there is a misconception here. In the Hebrew, it actually reads "line, line" it is not putting the lines on top of each other (line upon line). The Hebrew word that he uses for line is "**Qav,**" which means a cord or string that is used to **tie things together.** Isaiah is telling us (by inspiration from God) that we have to attach or tie the verses together. Then he says, "Here a little, and there a little," showing that we are taking verses from different locations in the Bible and attaching them together, little by little, until we get the deeper spiritual understanding of scripture. Those who are willing to learn, or already have this understanding, are going to be blessed beyond measure from this book.

After you understand all of that, there is still one important factor. The last component in opening up the spiritual understanding of scripture is the Holy Spirit. The Holy Spirit has to be active in our lives. In verse 11 and 12 of Isaiah 28 (posted on previous page), the writer speaks about stammering lips and another tongue. Then he says that God said, "This is the rest wherewith ye may cause the weary to rest." Paul confirms in 1 Cor 14:21-22 that the prophet was prophesying about the gift of tongues that came with the baptism of the Holy Spirit. The prophet is showing that not only do you have to know how to put the verses together and where to take the pieces of the puzzle from, but also the Holy Spirit is part of the equation. Everyone who is being called to salvation will have the Holy Spirit walking with them (and eventually in them). He is the Paraclete in Greek, which means the one who walks beside us. He plays the role of guiding us through scripture and the understanding of the Word. He opens up our understanding so that we can receive what God is saying in the Word of God. This is the same role Christ played (along with many others) when He walked with the disciples.

Luke 24:44-45
44 And he said unto them, These are the words which I spake unto you, while I was yet with you, that all things must be fulfilled, which were written in the law of Moses, and in the prophets, and in the psalms, concerning me.
45 **Then opened he their understanding, that they might understand the scriptures,**
KJV

The Father sends the Holy Spirit to walk with you long before He is in you. He is the one who opens up your understanding to the Gospel to save you. To understand scripture you have to get pieces from throughout the Bible and tie them together. The Holy Spirit not only guides you in finding the pieces but also shows you how to link them together. He also opens up your understanding so you know what they are saying spiritually.

I want to reiterate that this is why so many unbelievers think the Bible is foolishness. They cannot understand it. When I was a teenager I read the book of Revelation and before I was even done I threw it in a drawer, slammed it shut, and said, "These people crazy!" All I could see was beast coming out the earth, one third this, one fourth of that, seven of this, three of that, and nothing made any sense to me. Yet as a seasoned teacher in the Body of Christ today, all I can say is, "I can't wait for God to release me to write about Revelation." God gives the understanding of scripture through the Holy Spirit and those in Christ will receive disclosure on God's Word.

Over the years, I have taught the Bible to many people, which again is keeping with God's promise to me that I would be a teacher of many and they would know that I am a man of God. He also told me that my teachings would **bring people from where they are into His presence.** He has kept this promise and those who have read "The Truth about the Tithe" and "Assault on Innocence" my first two books would agree with me that I focus on entering and staying In Christ, which is to be in God's presence. His presence is that secret place.

Ps 91:1
91:1 He that dwelleth in **the secret place of the most High shall abide under the shadow of the Almighty.**
KJV

God's secret place is spiritual but the Garden of Eden was the manifestation of that secret place on the earth. His presence was in the Garden of Eden (the Paradise of God). I don't know where it is exactly, but the Holy Spirit showed me the gate to get there. This is my calling and I am going to show you what God has shown me about reaching the gate, the entrance to the Paradise of God. The story of the Garden of Eden is a dark saying that conceals the information. **The way to His presence is hidden in the Garden.**

Isa 57:17-21
17 For the iniquity of his covetousness was I wroth, and smote him: **I hid me**, and was wroth, and he went on frowardly in the way of his heart.
18 I have seen his ways, and will heal him: I will lead him also, and restore comforts unto him and to his mourners.
19 I create **the fruit of the lips**; Peace, peace to him that is far off, and to him that is near, saith the LORD; and I will heal him.
20 But the wicked are like the troubled sea, when it cannot rest, whose waters cast up mire and dirt.
21 There is no peace, saith my God, to the wicked.
KJV

I want you to read this excerpt from the book "The Assault on Innocence" carefully:

"Isaiah 57 verse 17 shows Adam's sin was covetousness (wanting something forbidden). God smote (cursed) Adam and all of humankind. God then shows that He hid Himself from humanity and allowed humankind to go forward walking in their own evil heart. God sees the evil that has overtaken humankind and decides to heal us. He sent Christ to pay the price for all humanity so that He could heal all those who accept the sacrifice. He is bringing them back into relationship with the Father by the Holy Spirit (the Comforter)."

What God has also done in secret is to have the writers of the Bible position the knowledge in it so that it conceals the full understanding from the wicked. **He hid the way to His presence in the scriptures.** God also used the same scriptures to hide or block the way back to His presence, from evil men. The Bible is literally written to turn all those who come to it with wrong intentions, or false beliefs that they are refusing to let go of, away from God's presence. **To those IN Christ He reveals His deep things by the Holy Spirit, allowing them entrance to His presence.** The Bible is a two-edged sword, it cuts both ways. It cuts you in and it cuts you out. The sword of the Spirit acts according to the intents of your heart.

Heb 4:12-13
12 For the word of God is quick, and powerful, and sharper than any twoedged sword, piercing even to the dividing asunder of soul and spirit, and of the joints and marrow, and is a discerner of the thoughts and intents of the heart.
13 Neither is there any creature that is not manifest in his sight: but all things are naked and opened unto the eyes of him with whom we have to do.
KJV

THE PUZZLE

Think of it as taking a puzzle and scattering it among the pages of a history book. God hid the puzzle among the events that are in the book. Your job is to go through all the pages of the book, secure all the pieces of the puzzle, and tie them together until you get the picture of what is really going on. **The history book tells you**

the natural events that took place but the puzzle tells you the spiritual events that are hidden between the lines.

Everyone can admit that the Bible is a book of historical events. The unbelievers may argue about its accuracy but we who have a relationship with God know it to be true. Yet beyond the natural understanding, there is a plethora (overabundance) of spiritual information that is mind blowing. The spiritual information is hidden in the book. In some cases, the pieces of the puzzle are camouflaged to fit exactly into the stories of the book even though they also carry a spiritual meaning. Yet some pieces do not fit the stories, if the reader is paying attention he will notice. Unbelievers cannot comprehend this and this is why the Bible says they cannot understand. The Word of God is foolishness to them. I always ask atheists how can you reject a book that you really do not understand. Take the greatest minds of the day and tell them to explain the simplest things in the Bible, not using the interpretations of others, and they cannot do it. The Bible attests to this fact:

1 Cor 1:23-29
23 But we preach Christ crucified, unto the Jews a stumblingblock, and unto the Greeks foolishness;
24 But unto them which are called, both Jews and Greeks, Christ the power of God, and the wisdom of God.
25 Because the foolishness of God is wiser than men; and the weakness of God is stronger than men.
26 For ye see your calling, brethren, how that not many wise men after the flesh, not many mighty, not many noble, are called:
27 But God hath chosen the foolish things of the world to confound the wise; and God hath chosen the weak things of the world to confound the things which are mighty;
28 And base things of the world, and things which are despised, hath God chosen, yea, and things which are not, to bring to nought things that are:
29 That no flesh should glory in his presence.
KJV

God could have chosen the wise, the famous, the handsome, or the rich to bring this revelation of His presence to the world. Instead, He chose me, someone who had no worthwhile achievements in this life until I came into relationship with God through Jesus Christ. Even my degrees were attained after I became a believer. I was a very smart child but there was no focus and no guidance. God came in and revealed to me that the abilities deposited in me from the womb were for His purpose. Until I came into relationship with Him, I was a boat with no sail, lost in the sea of a multitude of people. Thank God for God.

Dark Sayings

Unbelievers often come to me with the question, "Do you really believe in talking snakes?" When I explain to them that it was a serpent and the story is a dark saying that hides through metaphors the true identity of the serpent, they look at me puzzled. When I clarify it and explain who the serpent was in disguise I get silence from them. Their minds begin to churn, understanding that maybe there is something to the Bible.

Before we are done you will know exactly what and who the serpent was, and it sure was not a talking snake. Understanding the metaphors in the Garden is going to open up the understanding of the whole Bible. **The metaphors are the keys that open up doors of understanding. The Garden of Eden is full of golden keys.**

The objective is to get as many of these keys as you can and start opening up doors. Every door opens up to a room of learning where you will find at least one key and often multiple keys, which open other doors. Just before I started writing this book, God gave me a vision of a large group of gold keys on a key ring and one plugged into the internet outlet in my house. I received the interpretation that the internet was going to allow me to share the keys of understanding that God has given me.

I start a Facebook page for each book I write. I also have a discussion group open to the public that I run as a Bible study. These platforms allow me to distribute the keys of understanding. Please feel free to visit and like the page "Hidden in the Garden" and ask to be placed in the Bible study group in the comment section. I will be sharing the more than twenty five years of revelations freely to those in the group.

Remember that the keys are often metaphors that unlock the understanding of what God is saying in the scriptures. It is a hidden meaning or dark saying. It is like saying the person reading it is in the dark because they cannot understand the real meaning (unable to decipher the metaphors). Another word for these is parables, which are like riddles. God reveals to us that He normally speaks in dark sayings in scripture. This is brought to light in His dialogue about Moses:

Num 12:6-8

6 And he said, Hear now my words: If there be a prophet among you, **I the LORD will make myself known unto him in a vision, and will speak unto him in a dream.**

7 **My servant Moses is not so,** who is faithful in all mine house.

8 With him will **I speak mouth to mouth,** even apparently, and **not in dark speeches**; and the similitude of the LORD shall he behold: wherefore then were ye not afraid to speak against my servant Moses?

KJV

Because of Moses' faithfulness, God spoke to him plainly and did not hide anything from him. This is the same relationship that God has with Abraham because of his faithfulness.

Gen 18:17-19

17 And **the LORD said, Shall I hide from Abraham that thing which I do;**

18 Seeing that Abraham shall surely become a great and mighty nation, and all the nations of the earth shall be blessed in him?

19 For I know him, that he will command his children and his household after him, and they shall keep the way of the LORD, to do justice and judgment; that the LORD may bring upon Abraham that which he hath spoken of him.

KJV

Christ is the Word of God personified and just like God spoke in parables (dark sayings), Christ did also, and much of the Bible (the written Word of God) contains the same format. Christ confirms that dark sayings are parables to keep things secret when He quoted Ps 78:2-3 in Matt 13:35, which gives the understanding of what a dark saying actually means:

Matt 13:35
35 That it might be fulfilled which was spoken by the prophet, saying, I will open my mouth **in parables**; I will utter **things which have been kept secret** from the foundation of the world.
KJV

When you compare what He said with the verses below, you realize that dark sayings are used to keep hidden secret knowledge spoken from the foundation of the world. Christ spoke these things in His parables to reveal to those who believe, the truth hidden in scriptures:

Ps 78:2-3
2 I will open my mouth in a parable: I will utter **dark sayings of old**:
3 Which we have heard and known, and our fathers have told us.
KJV

A large percentage of the Bible contains the hidden wisdom of God and a carnal thinking person cannot understand it. Read what Paul is saying carefully:

1 Cor 2:7-14
7 But we speak **the wisdom of God in a mystery**, even the **hidden wisdom**, which **God ordained before the world unto our glory:**
8 Which none of the princes of this world knew: for had they known it, they would not have crucified the Lord of glory.
9 But as it is written, Eye hath not seen, nor ear heard, neither have entered into the heart of man, the things which God hath prepared for them that love him.
10 But **God hath revealed them unto us by his Spirit: for the Spirit searcheth all things, yea, the deep things** of God.
11 For what man knoweth the things of a man, save the spirit of man which is in him? Even so the things of God knoweth no man, but the Spirit of God.
12 Now we have received, not the spirit of the world, but the spirit which is of God; that we might know the things that are freely given to us of God.

13 Which things also we speak, **not in the words which man's wisdom teacheth, but which the Holy Ghost teacheth; comparing spiritual things with spiritual.**

14 But the natural man receiveth not the things of the Spirit of God: for **they are foolishness unto him: neither can he know them, because they are spiritually discerned.**

KJV

In verse 7, we read that God ordained for us to know this hidden wisdom. His Spirit teaches the deep things of God and only God can open up the understanding of a man to spiritual wisdom. You will find out that when God conceals a matter it is well hidden. **What is also going to shock you is that when God hides something, He often hides it right in plain sight.**

Prov 25:2

2 It is the glory of God to conceal a thing: but the honour of kings is to search out a matter.

KJV

God hid it for those who love Him to find it. Let's start this journey into the deeper things of God.

Amos 3:7

7 Surely the Lord GOD will do nothing, but **he revealeth his secret unto his servants the prophets.**

KJV

Parables

I want you to learn a little about parables. A parable is a story that uses metaphors to conceal the actual meaning. Here is an example: you can say trees when you are really speaking about angels. Therefore, you would replace the word angel with the word tree in the story. What is unique about Biblical metaphors is that once you understand what the metaphors represent you get a deeper spiritual understanding of the story. Those reading the story will think the writer is speaking about trees but those who understand the metaphor will know it is about angels. However, the more the hearer (or reader) understands about the functioning of trees, the more revelations they will receive on the purpose of the angels in the story. The metaphors in the Bible are two-edged. On one side they conceal the truth while on the other side they give a deeper understanding.

When most people think about parables in the Bible, they think about Christ's teachings in the gospels. Yet the Old Testament is full of parables. I want to share with you one parable spoken by God where the prophet speaking complains to God because the people do not understand him. God then gives the meaning of the parable by removing the metaphors and replacing the right names into the prophecy:

Ezek 20:46-49
46 Son of man, set thy face toward the **south**, and drop thy word toward the **south**, and prophesy against the **forest of the south field**;
47 And say to **the forest of the south**, Hear the word of the LORD; Thus saith the Lord GOD; Behold, **I will kindle a fire in thee**, and it **shall devour every green tree** in thee, and **every dry tree: the flaming flame shall not be quenched, and all faces from the south to the north shall be burned therein.**
48 And all flesh shall see that **I the LORD have kindled it: it shall not be quenched.**
49 Then said I, Ah Lord GOD! they say of me, **Doth he not speak parables?**
KJV

Just as the people Ezekiel were sent to, people reading this are saying, "What in the world is He talking about?" Now watch how God hears the plea of the prophet and then removes the dark saying and speaks clearly:

Ezek 21:1-5
21:1 And the word of the LORD came unto me, saying,
2 Son of man, set thy face toward **Jerusalem**, and drop thy word toward the **holy places**, and prophesy against the **land of Israel**,
3 And say to **the land of Israel**, Thus saith the LORD; Behold, **I am against thee, and will draw forth my sword out of his sheath,** and **will cut off from thee the righteous** and **the wicked.**

4 Seeing then that **I will cut off from thee the righteous and the wicked, therefore shall my sword go forth out of his sheath against all flesh from the south to the north:**
5 That all flesh may know that **I the LORD have drawn forth my sword out of his sheath: it shall not return any more.**
KJV

If you really can comprehend the simplicity of what God just did, then you have taken a big step in understanding the deeper things of God. Take a little time to compare the two groups of scriptures. Both groups of scriptures tell the exact same story. The first is written allegorically with metaphors, and the second is written plainly. Yes, I realize that some reading this will say, "They both look allegorical to me." LOL

What you just read has keys. "Keys that do what," you ask. The keys are to open doors of understanding, keys to cracking codes. Let's examine one of the keys. Verse 3 shows us that the metaphors for the righteous and the wicked are green tree and dry tree. Now we have the key understanding that when the Bible says green tree (metaphorically), it is speaking about righteous people and when it says dry tree it is speaking about wicked people. **Also, remember that just because God uses a word as a metaphor once, it does not mean every single time you see it in scripture it is a metaphor.** The Holy Spirit and experience will enable you to know when it is and when it is not. Now let's see what other doors this key will open:

Luke 23:28-31
28 But Jesus turning unto them said, Daughters of Jerusalem, weep not for me, but weep for yourselves, and for your children.
29 For, behold, the days are coming, in the which they shall say, Blessed are the barren, and the wombs that never bare, and the paps which never gave suck.
30 Then shall they begin to say to the mountains, Fall on us; and to the hills, Cover us.
31 For if they do these things in **a green tree**, what shall be **done in the dry?**
KJV

Christ is telling the Daughters of Jerusalem that if He is treated in such away as a righteous man, then what is going to happen to the wicked generation that has rejected Him. This is why He says they should be weeping for themselves.

Once we have the key of understanding that when the scriptures say green tree it means the righteous, and when it says dry tree it means the wicked, we can use that key to open up the understanding of other verses throughout the scriptures. When we understand what the metaphors mean, things start making sense.

Sidenote (very important): Did you notice that I did not use private interpretation (what I think it means) to get the understanding of what "Green tree" and "Dry tree" signify? Too many times, you will find ministers and scholars coming up with what makes sense according to their carnal mind of what the metaphor symbolizes. **YOU MUST NEVER DO THIS**. What makes sense to our carnal mind is often foolishness to God and totally at odds with spiritual understanding. This is a sure way of being lead astray into apostasy (false doctrine). Never interpret scripture; always allow the scriptures to interpret themselves. Every dark saying, parable, riddle, hidden wisdom, and question in scripture is answered **IN SCRIPTURE**. Again, let scripture interpret itself. If scripture gives a metaphor, find what it symbolizes by searching the scriptures with the assistance of the Holy Spirit. It might take a little time and effort but the answer will be there and it will be the correct answer.

2 Peter 1:20-21
20 Knowing this first, that **no prophecy of the scripture is of any private interpretation.**
21 For the prophecy came not in old time by the will of man: but holy men of God spake as they were moved by the Holy Ghost.
KJV

Brothers and sisters, we have some powerful revelations ahead of us in the coming chapters. I want to take up a little more space to prep you so that you can more easily understand how the metaphors and symbolisms work. This is not just important for you to understand this book but also for your spiritual life and growth. In Rev 3:18, Christ is giving a message to the Laodicean church, which many believe represent the church of today, the last generation. Christ uses many metaphors in this verse. He speaks of gold tested in the fire, white raiment, being clothed, nakedness, and eyesalve. Those are all metaphors. We are not going to review all of them for the sake of space, but if you want a complete breakdown read the last chapter of my book "The Truth About The Tithe." I do want to go into "gold tested in the fire" so you can get more practice on how metaphors work. When you have a full understanding on the workings of Biblical metaphors, it will make the steak (metaphor for knowledge) of the coming chapters easier to digest (understand). Yes, that was another metaphor. Below is an excerpt from my first book. It is repeating some of the points from earlier, but no worries, this will help to seal the understanding in your mind.

(Beginning of excerpt)
Rev 3:18
18 I counsel thee to buy of me **gold tried in the fire**, that thou mayest be rich; and white raiment, that thou mayest be clothed, and that the shame of thy nakedness do not appear; and anoint thine eyes with eyesalve, that thou mayest see.
KJV

Gold tried in the fire: To be rich
(What exactly is gold tried in the fire?)

Prov 17:3
3 The fining pot is for silver, and **the furnace for gold**: but the LORD trieth **the hearts**.
KJV

I understand that many people have been taught and believe that Christ is speaking of the Church going through the fire that they might be purified as gold. If you look closely at the verse you will realize that this is not what He is talking about at all. Christ said, **"Buy of me,"** meaning He is in possession of the gold that has already been tried in the fire. The gold has already been tested and He is the one who went through the fiery trials, tribulations, and suffering, to prove it is pure gold. Therefore, we come back to the question with a little more information. **What exactly is the gold tried in the fire that Christ possessed?**

Prov 25:11-12
11 **A word fitly spoken is like apples of gold** in pictures of silver.
12 As an earring of gold, and an ornament of fine gold, so is a wise
reprover upon an obedient ear.
KJV

**After you read the section below, please go back and read the
scripture above again.**

Let me give you a key. **Once again, a key is the
understanding of a metaphor used in scripture.** It is an
instrument of knowledge that unlocks the meaning of a parable or
dark saying of God. There are tons of knowledge locked up in the
Bible and the mistake most people make is looking for the key to
unlocking the knowledge outside of the Bible. That is what Peter
meant when he said the prophecy of the scripture should not be
understood through private interpretation. If you want to know what
the metaphor for gold means, it will be found in the scripture. **Once
you find the key understanding, it will open up the meaning of
many other verses.**

**Any time I am looking for the key understanding of a
metaphor in the Bible, the first book I go to is "Proverbs."
Solomon wrote Proverbs specifically to give knowledge,
understanding, and wisdom to the reader.** Proverbs also shines
the light on the metaphors in scripture and many people miss this
fact. I want you to read the first six verses of Proverbs carefully!

Prov 1:1-6
1:1 The proverbs of Solomon the son of David, king of Israel;
2 **To know wisdom** and instruction; to perceive **the words of
understanding;**
3 To receive the instruction of wisdom, justice, and judgment, and
equity;
4 To give subtilty to the simple, to the young man knowledge and
discretion.
5 **A wise man will hear, and will increase learning**; and a man of
understanding shall attain unto wise counsels:
6 **To understand a proverb, and the interpretation; the words of
the wise, and their dark sayings.** KJV

Note to readers: "Dark sayings" are not something negative but means that the understanding is hidden, as in a parable or riddle. Proverbs shines the light (gives understanding) on dark sayings!

Teacher's Anointing

Understanding is the silver and wisdom is the gold. After God anointed me as a teacher in the Body of Christ, He gave me a dream/vision of a big box the size of a coffee table. It looked like a big jewelry box. The box did not open from the top; it had slim, elongated drawers that slid out towards the front, one upon another, from the top to the bottom. I looked into two or three of the drawers and they were filled with gemstones. Each drawer had gems of the same color and type (for example, one drawer all rubies; one all diamonds; another all sapphires). The gems were different sizes and they were placed in the drawer in the pattern of a dartboard lying flat. The bulls-eye would always contain the biggest gem. Those drawers of gems represented different types of wisdom. In addition, the biggest gem in the middle was the key area of wisdom that linked all the rest. It is one of the most beautiful things God has shown me.

The revelation was that believers are the jewelry boxes and if you allow the Holy Spirit to teach you, your box will be full:

Prov 20:15
15 There is gold, and a multitude of rubies: but **the lips of knowledge are a precious jewel.**
KJV

People have misconstrued multitudes of verses in the Bible speaking about people of God being rich, as pertaining only to carnal things, when the majority of times it's pertaining to spiritual riches. The example God gives us of the perfect church, Smyrna, is that they were poor in carnal things but rich in the spiritual things of God. Their jewelry boxes were full:

Rev 2:9
9 I know thy works, and tribulation, and poverty, (but thou art rich)...
(KJV)

In Laodicea, you find a church speaking of all they have, as if gain means godliness, which Paul warned us about in 1 Tim 6. In the things of this world they were rich, but in spiritual things, their jewelry boxes were full of dust and cobwebs. Yet Christ had appointed an angel over each church and this shows they had access to Christ's treasure house. Do you realize that God's wisdom is like a treasure house? When Christ opens His mouth, He is giving us access to silver, gold, and precious jewels. Moreover, His gold was tested in the fiery trials He went through to prove it was pure gold:

Prov 16:16
16 **How much better is it to get wisdom than gold**! and to get understanding rather to be chosen than silver!
KJV

Fruit of the lips is wisdom (important for later).

Prov 8:19
19 **My fruit is better than gold,** yea, than fine gold; and my revenue than choice silver.
KJV

Therefore, when Christ told the Laodicea church to come and buy gold tested in the fire so they might be rich, He was telling them to come to Him and buy wisdom that had been tested. It took Him through the suffering, trials, and tribulations of the cross and showed through His resurrection that it was **true wisdom.** Christ's wisdom was pure gold sent down by the Father from heaven. **We have to hold on to this truth that real riches are with God and they are accessed through Christ.** These treasures do not perish like those of this world.

Now we understand the revelation that the gold tested in the fire comes from Christ and is a metaphor for wisdom.
(End of excerpt)

The more God can trust us to walk in righteousness and do what is right, the more He reveals to us. The key is to learn how to operate in love, which is to put on the image of Christ.

I want you take a couple seconds, walk away from the book, and pray that God would open up your understanding, then come back and read the verses below carefully.

Prov 8:22-36

22 The LORD possessed me in the beginning of his way, before his works of old.

23 I was set up **from everlasting,** from the beginning, or ever the earth was.

24 When there were no depths, **I was brought forth;** when there were no fountains abounding with water.

25 Before the mountains were settled, before the hills was **I brought forth:**

26 While as yet he had not made the earth, nor the fields, nor the highest part of the dust of the world.

27 When he prepared the heavens, I was there: when he set a compass upon the face of the depth:

28 When he established the clouds above: when he strengthened the fountains of the deep:

29 When he gave to the sea his decree, that the waters should not pass his commandment: when he appointed the foundations of the earth:

30 **Then I was by him, as one brought up with him:** and I was daily his delight, rejoicing always before him;

31 **Rejoicing in the habitable part of his earth;** and my delights were with the sons of men.

32 Now therefore hearken unto me, O ye children: for blessed are they that keep my ways.

33 Hear instruction, and be wise, and refuse it not.

34 Blessed is the man that **heareth me, watching daily at my gates, waiting at the posts of my doors.**

35 For whoso **findeth me findeth life,** and shall obtain favour of the LORD.

36 But he that sinneth against me wrongeth his own soul: **all they that hate me love death.**

KJV

The above verses are very powerful and the revelation hidden in them is that the chapter, which is speaking about wisdom, is actually speaking about Christ. The one spoken about by the name of Wisdom is actually Jesus Christ. **Christ is Wisdom.** We recognize Him as Wisdom not only when we understand the characteristics of the one being spoken about can only match up to Christ but scripture also identifies Him as the Wisdom of God. (Precept upon precept, line line, here a little, there a little.)

1 Cor 1:24
24 But unto them which are called, both Jews and Greeks, Christ the power of God, and **the wisdom of God**.
KJV

Please read the verses from Prov 8: 22-36 one more time. Much of what is going to be revealed to you in the rest of the book is hidden in those verses.

Chapter 2

The Talents

Why is comprehending metaphors, which increases our understanding of the Bible, so important? Knowledge, wisdom, and understanding of the things of God are all we can take with us from this life. We cannot take the car, the house, or the money in the bank but what God deposits in us will leave with us. It will not only determine if we attain eternal life but also will determine our status in the next life, eternally in God's Kingdom. Do you realize that the very angels in heaven study and have different levels of understanding of the Word of God? Pay attention to Gabriel's testimony:

Dan 10:20-21
20 Then said he, Knowest thou wherefore I come unto thee? and now will I return to fight with the prince of Persia: and when I am gone forth, lo, the prince of Grecia shall come.
21 But **I will shew thee that which is noted in the scripture of truth: and there is none that holdeth with me in these things, but Michael your prince.**
KJV

If the very angels see the wisdom in studying the Word of Truth, then how beneficial do you think it will be to us?

Pay attention closely. **Knowledge comprehended equals understanding. When we know how to apply this understanding properly, it equals wisdom.** Do you realize that you can have all the information on a subject (knowledge) yet do not have the understanding of how it works? Other times you will have the knowledge and understanding but do not have the ability to apply it. There have also been times when I have had the knowledge of something and the understanding of how it works. Yet, even with the knowledge and understanding, I did not know how to apply it to my life. In this area, I lacked wisdom.

When I first found out about fasting, I had the knowledge of it being no calorie intake. I knew that it helped us in our spiritual walk and was necessary for spiritual growth. Yet I still did not know how it actually worked. I did not understand what actually happens when we fast. I started with the knowledge, but was not aware of the spiritual mechanics of it. When the Holy Spirit opened up my understanding and showed me what takes place in the spirit realm when we are fasting properly, I finally understood the spiritual workings of the fast. I attained the understanding so I could properly utilize the knowledge of fasting. (See the chapter on fasting in "Assault on Innocence" volume 1.) Yet, I did not have the wisdom on how to properly apply the fast and utilize it to defeat the enemy. I later learned that fasting was to be utilized to petition God for guidance. This goes beyond the basic knowledge of fasting. When you apply the knowledge in the proper manner, it becomes wisdom. **You do not fast to move God, You fast to hear God.** You do not fast to tell God what you need Him to do. **You fast to quiet the flesh so you can hear clearly, what God needs you to do.** That is the wisdom of fasting. When you apply the wisdom of fasting to the knowledge and understanding, then your fasting becomes powerful.

Every person that believes that Christ Jesus is the Word of God sent by the Father into the world, in the flesh, and He is the Messiah sent to die for our sins, is brought back into relationship with God. You become a believer when you accept this truth. Christ came in the flesh with instructions from the Father for every believer under the New Covenant. Every believer is deposited with an initial Word of God. Christ was sent with this knowledge, understanding, and wisdom. It is the bread of life. It is the living water. It is the wine. The bread of life is the knowledge sent to us from God. The living water is the Holy Spirit's understanding of the things of God given to us. The wine is the wisdom of God poured into us. Now what do you do with it? You have to trade it. What? You don't believe me? Let's ask Christ.

Let me share a short testimony before we get into what Christ said. I remember hearing a sermon preached on the parable of the talents where the preacher thought a talent meant a person having talents like dancing or singing. The church was cheering as the charismatic preacher poured out his (seemed to be) powerful message on how God can increase your talents (preaching, dancing, singing, etc.) so you can be a blessing to the body. It was a lack of understanding, yet the church was moved by the fact that the preacher was a great orator (speaker). They received wood that day and thought it was silver and gold (talent) because the speaker did not realize that a talent in the Bible is actually a measure of weight of silver or gold utilized as money.

Talanton
NT:5007 talanton (tal'-an-ton); neuter of a presumed derivative of the original form of tlao (to bear; equivalent to NT:5342); a balance (as supporting weights), i.e. (by implication) a certain weight (and thence a coin or rather sum of money) or "talent":KJV - talent.
(Biblesoft's New Exhaustive Strong's Numbers and Concordance)

It is not the ability to sing well. The sad fact is that things like this happen countless of times in today's churches where many are looking to be emotionally moved and entertained instead of moved by a true Word of God, which comes with power to change lives. Church is not about a quick fix from an emotionally charged message with no sustenance. **It is a place that contains a storehouse of the things of God set away to be deposited in those that believe and to call and convert the unbeliever.** We are to leave with more of the things of God than what we came with. It is a place of increase in the mysteries of the Kingdom. Now let's get well feed!

Christ's message

Matt 25:14-30
14 For the kingdom of heaven is as **a man** travelling into a far country, who called his own servants, and delivered unto them his goods.

15 And unto one he gave five talents, to another two, and to another one; to every man **according to his several ability**; and straightway took his journey.

16 Then he that had received the five talents went and **traded with the same,** and made them other five talents.

17 And likewise he that had received two, he also gained other two.

18 But he that had received one went and **digged in the earth, and hid his lord's money.**

19 After a long time the lord of those servants cometh, and reckoneth with them.

20 And so he that had received five talents came and brought other five talents, saying, Lord, thou deliveredst unto me five talents: behold, I have gained beside them five talents more.

21 His lord said unto him, Well done, thou good and faithful servant: thou hast been faithful over a few things, I will make thee ruler over many things: enter thou into the joy of thy lord.

22 He also that had received two talents came and said, Lord, thou deliveredst unto me two talents: behold, I have gained two other talents beside them.

23 His lord said unto him, Well done, good and faithful servant; thou hast been faithful over a few things, I will make thee ruler over many things: enter thou into the joy of thy lord.

24 Then he which had received the one talent came and said, Lord, I knew thee that thou art an hard man, reaping where thou hast not sown, and gathering where thou hast not strawed:

25 And I was afraid, and went and hid thy talent in the earth: lo, there thou hast that is thine.

26 His lord answered and said unto him, Thou wicked and slothful servant, thou knewest that I reap where I sowed not, and gather where I have not strawed:

27 Thou oughtest therefore to have put **my money to the exchangers**, and then at my coming I should have received mine own with usury.

28 Take therefore the talent from him, and give it unto him which hath ten talents.

29 **For unto every one that hath shall be given, and he shall have abundance: but from him that hath not shall be taken away even that which he hath.**

30 And cast ye the unprofitable servant into outer darkness: there shall be weeping and gnashing of teeth. KJV

Now we know Christ is telling a parable and as we have learned earlier, it contains a hidden message. If you understand the metaphors, you will understand the message. Christ often talks about the Kingdom of heaven and likens it to some circumstance here on earth to reveal the hidden knowledge and wisdom of the Kingdom. We first realize that the man that is leaving to go into a far country is Christ Himself leaving to go back to the Father. In the parable, the man that represents Christ distributes to each of His servants goods that do not belong to the servants but to the man who is the master. In the same way, Christ has left, or more accurately, deposited into every believer who will accept Him. In the parable, the talent is money, which consists of a weight of gold or silver. As we saw earlier, the money represents the knowledge, understanding, and wisdom of the kingdom.

Prov 8:10-21

10 **Receive my instruction, and not silver; and knowledge rather than choice gold.**

11 **For wisdom is better than rubies**; and all the things that may be desired are not to be compared to it.

12 **I wisdom** dwell with prudence, and find out **knowledge** of witty inventions.

13 The **fear of the LORD** is to hate evil: pride, and arrogancy, and the evil way, and the froward mouth, do I hate.

14 **Counsel** is mine, and **sound wisdom**: I am **understanding**; I have **strength**.

15 By me kings reign, and princes decree justice.

16 By me princes rule, and nobles, even all the judges of the earth.

17 I love them that love me; and those that seek me early shall find me.

18 Riches and honour are with me; yea, durable riches and righteousness.

19 **My fruit is better than gold, yea, than fine gold; and my revenue than choice silver.**

20 I lead in the way of righteousness, in the midst of the paths of judgment:

21 That I may cause those that love me to inherit substance; and I will fill their treasures.

KJV

Prov 16:16
16 **How much better is it to get wisdom than gold! and to get understanding rather to be chosen than silver!**
KJV

Each servant received an amount according to his ability. The Greek word that is translated ability is "dunamis," which means force or power. In "Assault on Innocence," I share the revelation that there are different levels of grace and the higher the level of grace, the more power we have in our personal lives and ministry. This is why Christ told Paul that His grace was sufficient for Paul to overcome the thorn in his flesh. **The level of grace we receive is according to our humility. Humility determines grace and the level of grace determines power:**

2 Cor 12:9-10
9 And he said unto me, **My grace is sufficient for thee: for my strength is made perfect in weakness.** Most gladly therefore will I rather glory in my infirmities, **that the power of Christ may rest upon me.**
10 Therefore I take pleasure in infirmities, in reproaches, in necessities, in persecutions, in distresses for Christ's sake: for **when I am weak, then am I strong.**
KJV

This is why God takes us through so much; He is trying to humble us because the strength of God operates in us according to our level of humility. In addition, the more knowledge we receive the more humble we have to be least we get caught up in pride. The difference between the three servants was their ability, which was their power or force. It was their level of humility that determined how much spiritual money (knowledge) they received.

James 4:6-7
6 But he **giveth more grace.** Wherefore he saith, **God resisteth the proud, but giveth grace unto the humble.**
7 Submit yourselves therefore to God. Resist the devil, and he will flee from you.
KJV

When we submit to God, it means we humble ourselves before Him. We follow the example Christ left us.

Luke 22:42
42 Saying, Father, if thou be willing, remove this cup from me: nevertheless not my will, but thine, be done.
KJV

Submitting to God's will is an act of humility, which allows us access to the power given to us by the level of grace God gave us. When Christ told Paul "My grace is sufficient," He was letting Paul know he had access to enough power to resist the devil and make him flee but he would only access the fullness of the power when he was weak by walking in humility.

The servant's responsibility is to increase in the knowledge, understanding, and wisdom of the Kingdom. This is the talent that was left in their possession. Christ confirms that the mysteries of the Kingdom are the talents:

Matt 13:11-12
11 He answered and said unto them, Because it is given unto you to know **the mysteries of the kingdom of heaven**, but to them it is not given.
12 For **whosoever hath, to him shall be given, and he shall have more abundance: but whosoever hath not, from him shall be taken away even that he hath.**
KJV

We as believers have the knowledge of God deposited in us. How do we increase this knowledge? The servant who received the five talents states that he traded with it. In the normal sense of the matter, we understand that when you trade you give up to get. However, what is so powerful about the story is that both wise servants gave to get without losing any of what they initially invested. This is the way of the Kingdom. When two believers sit down and discuss Biblical matters, they are exchanging what they know about the things of God. Nevertheless, the knowledge you arrived with is not lost though you gain new knowledge from the discussion.

It is as if we both have different clues to find a hidden treasure. We realize that the treasure is an endless supply so it is enough for both parties. We sit down and reveal the clues we have to each other realizing that I have some clues the same as yours, some different, and vise versa. When we get up and leave, we will have both exchanged clues to find the treasure but we also maintain the clues we came with. I leave with my knowledge, which has increased because I have acquired yours and you are the same having acquired mine. **Remember that the only thing we can take with us when we leave this world is what we know and the only thing worth anything in the spirit realm is Kingdom knowledge.** When we are active in the things of God interacting with the people of God, we increase the knowledge of God deposited in us.

This is why it is so important to surround ourselves with people of God who are seeking the deeper things of the Kingdom and not with people seeking the things of this world. There is a treasure house full of the understanding of the things of the Kingdom deposited in the children of God. Those walking in humility and seeking first the Kingdom of heaven and His righteousness are going to be full. God reveals the mysteries to those seeking after Him and when we fellowship one with another and share our testimonies we increase in Kingdom money. We increase what Christ has deposited in us. We wait joyfully for His return because we know we have increased His goods.

1 Cor 2:6-7
6 Howbeit we speak wisdom among them that are perfect: **yet not the wisdom of this world**, nor of the princes of this world, that come to nought:
7 But **we speak the wisdom of God in a mystery,** even **the hidden wisdom,** which God ordained before the world unto our glory:
KJV

Now we come to the wicked servant that took the money (knowledge) deposited in him and buried it in the dirt. We realize why he only received one talent, because the dialogue exposes that he is a prideful and rude servant. Have you ever spoken to a Christian that talked as if God owes them something? Every conversation is about what they can get or about why things need to go their way.

What is the problem? You are not increasing in the knowledge, wisdom, and understanding of God. What is the issue? You are spending your time with the things of this world, exchanging knowledge in the ways of this world. You have buried the knowledge of God under the spiritually worthless knowledge of this world. What is the solution? Dig up the knowledge of God deposited in you. Surround your self with the things and people of God and trade the knowledge that you have. Attain more of what is from God so that you can present gain to Christ upon His return.

The gaining of knowledge can be instantaneous and can also come through experience. The key is to reinforce in our minds that we have to gain the knowledge. We have to add to what God has given us. The parable shows that this is mandatory.

Christ even explains to the servant that if he would have taken the money and given it to the exchangers (bank) that it would have gained interest on its own and He would have gotten gain. The word used in the Greek for exchangers or bank is *trapeza*, which literally means a table. It is the table where the exchanges take place. Remember that Kingdom money is God's knowledge and just like when we go to the bank (or the exchangers table) to do business and allow them to lend our money for interest, the same can be done with God's money. The question is, does God have a table where He shares knowledge?

Prov 9:1-11

9:1 **Wisdom hath builded her house,** she hath hewn out her seven pillars:

2 She hath killed her beasts; **she hath mingled her wine; she hath also furnished her table.**

3 She hath sent forth her maidens: she crieth upon the highest places of the city,

4 Whoso is simple, let him turn in hither: as for him that wanteth understanding, she saith to him,

5 **Come, eat of my bread, and drink of the wine which I have mingled.**

6 **Forsake the foolish, and live; and go in the way of understanding.**

7 He that reproveth a scorner getteth to himself shame: and he that rebuketh a wicked man getteth himself a blot.

8 Reprove not a scorner, lest he hate thee: rebuke a wise man, and he will love thee.

9 **Give instruction to a wise man, and he will be yet wiser: teach a just man, and he will increase in learning.**

10 **The fear of the LORD is the beginning of wisdom: and the knowledge of the holy is understanding.**

11 **For by me thy days shall be multiplied, and the years of thy life shall be increased.**

KJV

Do you see it? It is God's house. Bring what you have to God's house and it will increase. I am not talking about every church because many churches have little to do with God and the presence of God is not there. I am talking about true places of God, to include small gatherings, where the Spirit of God is operating.

When you read the scripture above you may wonder where is this house that wisdom has built. Once again, understand that the metaphors open up the meaning of the proverb. **God's wisdom is always Christ, whether it is referred to as a woman or a man. The Word of God is the Wisdom of God.**

The seven pillars represent the seven angels or seven Spirits of God (Rev 1:4). The seven Spirits of God are represented by the Menorah the seven-headed lamp stand (EX 25:30-37) that sits in the Holy Place of God's Temple. **This is God's anointing and His wine.**

The table that has been furnished is symbolized by the table of shewbread that also sits in the Holy Place of the Temple across from the Menorah (lamp stand). These sit right before the vail that covers the entrance into the Holy of Holies where the mercy seat sits on the ark with the two cherubim angels and God's presence called the Shepherd of Israel in scripture.

There are churches that dwell in the Holy Place where the anointing of God is flowing through His Spirit and the seven Spirits of God. This is where the shewbread is on the table, which is the knowledge of the mysteries of the Kingdom. There are also churches set up to manipulate and feed off the sheep instead of feeding them. As we draw closer to God, He will draw us away from these places.

Therefore, when Christ told the servant that he should have gone to the exchangers, He was telling us that if we go to the place of God, our knowledge of God will increase. Yet, we can see by Proverbs 9 that it has to be a place in connection with God that sits before the Holy of Holies, which makes it a Holy Place where the shewbread (knowledge of God) and the lamp stand (the anointed oil of God) is in operation. Some Christians are too lazy to go on their own and participate in the spreading of the Gospel of God. Then even when it comes to attending the places, where God's presence is, to sit and listen to the things of God that is too much to ask also. These people are servants of God, but just like the wicked servant, they will be thrown into outer darkness.

We as believers must not be fooled by a facade. Just because a place looks holy does not mean that it is the Holy Place. When you leave your church, do you feel like someone has poured into you things you did not know, or do you feel like you have been well entertained? Is the majority of the preaching about the Kingdom or about living in this world? Is the anointing of God operating with healings and deliverance or are you receiving motivational speeches to make self feel better? If your talents (understanding of the mysteries of the Kingdom) are not increasing, then you might be enjoying yourself but you are just wasting time. You have unknowingly buried your talents.

As believers, we go through a process of progression that leads us to two things: Loving God and loving one another. The mysteries of the Kingdom all point to this ending. The knowledge of the Kingdom expounds on everything from our start in faith, to our end in love, and everything in between. That is the purpose of this knowledge because everything from faith to love (and all between) equals righteousness. Peter himself confirmed this process of progression:

(Love = charity)

2 Peter 1:4-11

4 Whereby are given unto us exceeding great and precious promises: that by these ye might be partakers of the divine nature, having escaped the corruption that is in the world through lust.

5 And beside this, giving all diligence, add to your **faith virtue**; and to **virtue knowledge**;

6 And to **knowledge temperance**; and to **temperance patience**; and to **patience godliness**;

7 And to **godliness brotherly kindness**; and to **brotherly kindness charity.**

8 For if these things be in you, and abound, they make you that **ye shall neither be barren nor unfruitful in the knowledge of our Lord Jesus Christ.**

9 But he that lacketh these things is blind, and cannot see afar off, and hath forgotten that he was purged from his old sins.

10 Wherefore the rather, brethren, give diligence to make your calling and election sure: for if ye do these things, ye shall never fall:

11 For so **an entrance shall be ministered unto you abundantly into the everlasting kingdom of our Lord and Saviour Jesus Christ.**

KJV

The mysteries of the Kingdom point us to the Law of the Kingdom, which is summed up in loving one another and loving God. By learning the mysteries of the Kingdom and then applying the lessons taught in them to our lives, we become not just hearers of the Word but doers also. **We cannot be in this just to attain the knowledge because it cannot bring about change in us if we do not apply it.**

1 Cor 13:2

2 And though I have the gift of prophecy, and understand all mysteries, and all knowledge; and though I have all faith, so that I could remove mountains, and have not charity, I am nothing.

KJV

Ok, we're ready. You might want to get some snacks, a beverage, and strap yourself in because we are about to enter the Garden.

Chapter 3

The Fruit Is The Key

Prov 18:21
21 Death and life are in the power of the tongue: and they that love it shall eat the fruit thereof.
KJV

It was in my early years of teaching Bible study when God instructed me to get the core of the Bible study group and start meeting during the week for prayer. There were seven of us meeting at the home of one of the members. All of us had received the baptism of the Holy Spirit and were operating in the gifts. Some of the most powerful manifestations of the gifts of God took place in those meetings. The visions we were having were extremely intense. I remember God showing me a wall in a vision that was so high and wide that I could not see where it ended. More amazingly, I could touch the wall with my mind and actually feel it standing before me. I literally felt the crevices, the texture, and the matter with my mind. It was as real as can be, even though it was a vision.

We were being taught and some of the lessons were hard and heavy. There were also many spiritual attacks from the enemy in an attempt to hinder what God was doing with us. The fights we went through were my first introductions into how the enemy will attempt to break up groups of people gathered together to grow spiritually in the things of God. Yet God kept us through that season and continued to open our understanding of the scriptures.

One Thursday night, as we sat at the dining room table talking, the presence of God entered the room. One of the members started speaking in tongues and I was shocked when the interpretation came. The interpretation made no sense and I was ready to rebuke it. Here is the kicker. I am the one who brought the interpretation. Now during interpretation the Holy Spirit will have you speak in English what He spoke in tongues. It is not a word-for-word translation, but you speak the interpretation of the message. What did I speak? "The fruit the fruit, the fruit is the key." After I spoke it, I thought to myself, "What?" As I looked around the room, the others were looking at me in anticipation of the rest of the message. However, nothing else came. That was it. **"The fruit the fruit, the fruit is the key."**

I left there a little disappointed and confused because none of us knew what it meant. It was a Thursday night, so I had to go to work. I carried a little pocket Bible with me wherever I went. I was working at the time as a correctional sergeant for the Department of Corrections, in Florida. I was assigned to a dormitory with an officer working under my supervision on the night shift. This gave me the opportunity to do some reading between counts and other duties in the dorm.

The Holy Spirit took over as soon as I opened the scriptures and started taking me through the correct understanding of what the fruit was that was eaten in the Garden. It happened quickly. I was turning the pages as if it were a lesson I had studied for countless years. Precept upon precept, precept upon precept. Line line, line line. Here a little, there a little, and then it was done. I understood exactly what I was being shown and I wanted to scream.

I was about to burst with this new information and I needed to vent it. I have a close friend who was a fellow sergeant at the institution named Ivory; I called and asked him if he could come to the dorm. I could not even wait; I exited the dorm to go get him. As I exited the fence of my dormitory and started walking towards the movement control building, the door opened and he existed. I said to him, "God showed me what the fruit in the Garden is." We stood outside, then I started rambling off the verses to him, and all he could respond with was, "Wow!" We looked at each other and literally started running around praising God. We immediately understood how powerful the revelation was and that the fruit was the key to opening up a deeper understanding into the Garden of Eden. Yet, I still did not grasp how deep this was going to take me in comprehending the deeper things of God. I was opening the door to a room full of wonderful understandings and before I could even get the door fully open, the brightness from the light inside was beaming out. Glory be to God. **The fruit was the key!**

This is the revelation. When Christians think of the metaphor of fruit, the first thing that comes to mind is the fruit of the Spirit or the fruit of your doings (actions). These are correct interpretations of the meaning of fruit in the scriptures but they are not the only ones. What was revealed to me was that the first time the metaphor is used, which was in the Garden, it is speaking of the fruit of your lips. What we speak out of our mouths are also fruit. I want you to think of it like this: the fruit is the story and the theme of the story is the seed contained in the fruit. The message of the words is the seed contained in the story being told. When people ingest the fruit, they also consume the hidden seed in the fruit. This book is a fruit and the theme of the book (understanding the hidden knowledge from the Garden) is the seed in the fruit. **Adam and Eve did not eat a natural fruit such as an apple. They consumed spoken knowledge with the theme that they could be their own gods. Let's get these pieces to the puzzle.**

Death and life - the two trees

Very often, we hear that death and life are in the power of the tongue. This is a very powerful verse and a true saying. We are told that with our tongues, we can speak death or we can speak life and this is truth. How many times have you heard someone quote the rest of the verse? "And those that love it shall eat the fruit thereof." See, the death and life in the verse is speaking about something specific. The two trees in the garden are the tree of life and the tree of knowledge of good and evil that causes death. The tree is the tree of death (there is another name but that is for later). The tree of death kills by corrupt knowledge. It is the cyanide mixed into the Kool-Aid; death by ingesting a poisonous mix of good and evil.

Now, let's read the verse again with the previous verse for clarification.

Prov 18:20-21
20 A man's belly shall be satisfied with **the fruit of his mouth**; and with **the increase of his lips** shall he be filled.
21 **Death and life** are in **the power of the tongue**: and they that love it shall eat **the fruit** thereof.
KJV

You can ingest knowledge. Whatever you love, whether death or life, will be what you ingest. Spoken words are going to go down into your belly. It will give you death or life because you will be eating from one of the trees. **The belly is a metaphor for the soul.** Spoken words cause the transformation of our souls, which will take on the image of life or the image of death according to the words we are ingesting.

Prov 18:8
8 The words of a talebearer are as wounds, and **they go down into the innermost parts of the belly.**
KJV

There has never been an autopsy that found a stomach full of words. The words go down into the innermost parts of our souls and cause wounds of hurt when people speak lies against us.

Christ gave us the key, but are we paying attention?

Luke 6:43-45
43 For a good tree bringeth not forth **corrupt fruit**; neither doth a corrupt tree bring forth **good fruit**.
44 For **every tree is known by his own fruit**. For of thorns men do not gather figs, nor of a bramble bush gather they grapes.
45 A good man out of the good treasure of his heart bringeth forth that which is good; and an evil man out of the evil treasure of his heart bringeth forth that which is evil: **for of the abundance of the heart his mouth speaketh.**
KJV

The abundance of your heart identifies the fruit you speak out of your mouth. Again, Christ confirms the fruit is spoken words:

Matt 12:33-37
33 Either make **the tree good, and his fruit good**; or else make **the tree corrupt, and his fruit corrupt**: for the tree is known by his fruit.
34 O generation of vipers, **how can ye, being evil, speak good things?** For out of **the abundance of the heart the mouth speaketh.**
35 A good man out of the good treasure of the heart bringeth forth good things: and an evil man out of the evil treasure bringeth forth evil things.
36 But I say unto you, **That every idle word that men shall speak, they shall give account thereof in the day of judgment.**
37 **For by thy words thou shalt be justified, and by thy words thou shalt be condemned.**
KJV

God hides things out in the open because many a year I have read those scriptures and missed that Christ was saying that your words are the fruit of the lips. Yet here is the power in the Word of God. It can hide a matter from you and yet when the Holy Spirit is ready to open up your understanding, you find the answer right in front of you. God told us in the Garden that the fruit was spoken words. We all missed it. Read this carefully:

Gen 3:10-11
10 And he said, I heard thy voice in the garden, and I was afraid, because I was naked; and I hid myself.
11 And he said, **Who told thee** that thou wast naked? **Hast thou eaten of the tree**, whereof I commanded thee that thou shouldest not eat?
KJV

God says plainly that to eat from the tree is to be told something, and we all missed it.

Seed hidden in the fruit

I want to give you a deeper understanding of how the fruit works. The fruit is symbolic of a message that contains words that can come by conversation, book, movie, play, video, song, etc. You have bland fruits, you have sour fruits, but most are sweet. A fruit is made so that those who will consume it will take it with the seed that is hidden in it. Some seeds are so small that when an animal consumes them they do not even notice the seed, which is ingested with the fruit. We can call these subliminal messages. Other seeds are so large that to ingest them is a slow process but when we carry away the fruit, we take the seed. These are mysteries and dark sayings. Whether taken or ingested the seed will be distributed to another area where it is hopeful to find fertile ground to reproduce its kind. When the fruit is a song, not everyone will like the genre but those who do (love it) will listen to the song (eat the fruit), and the theme of the song (seed) will be planted in their soul and start to grow until it bears its own fruit. You then begin to sing the song (fruit of your lips). **Here is where the end danger comes in. We sign contracts or covenants with our mouths.** If you confess it then a spirit has authority to enter you and bring it about. Example: Your daughter is listening to a song titled, "I kissed a girl and I liked it." As she ingests the song and the theme of lesbianism is planted in her soul, then she starts singing the song and states, "I kissed a girl and I liked it." As soon as she confesses that, there will be a spirit that is going to enter in with the authority to make what she confessed happen. Now do you understand how dangerous corrupt fruits are? (For more information on how the enemy entraps us through what we confess, please see the series **"Assault on Innocence."**)

Adam was made from the dirt of the ground. When we take a natural seed and place it in dirt, it germinates and starts to grow. In the spiritual, when we take the seed of a message (either life or death) and place it within us, it germinates in our souls and starts to grow. A seed puts down roots first, which starts the transformation of the median it is set in (soul), and then absorbs it by breaking it down and transforming it into the tree, which the fruit came from. Seeds reproduce after their kind. Trees of life have fruit that contain seeds that produce trees of life. Trees of death have fruit that contain seeds that produce trees of death. Trees of life are assigned to eternal life, and trees of death are assigned to eternal death (separation from God) and damnation.

Just because you ingest the wrong seed does not mean it is over but the longer you let the seed stay in the ground the harder it will be to uproot it. Sometimes, we as Christians find ourselves in places where evil seeds are being cast around and we think we can avoid them.

In nature, there are seeds that are so small that many of us would need a magnifying glass to see them clearly. Spiritually these small seeds are like subliminal messages and they are effective. When a company pays 5 million dollars for a 30-second commercial in the Super Bowl, they are not paying that kind of money for something that does not work. It is a proven fact that people watch, listen, and react to the commercials. The more mess we have in our heart, the more it becomes like a vineyard filled with weeds and the easier it is for the enemy to throw in some seeds of death that we are unable to see. Then you are in the store buying a product because you saw it in a 30 seconds commercial. If 30 seconds can make a person buy a product, **what can a two-hour movie do?**

We talked earlier about the things of this world can be symbolized as dirt. It is easy to take a seed, place it in the dirt of our hearts, and cover it. If I hid some seeds in the dirt of my backyard and sent you out to find them, it would be almost impossible without serious help. Most times, we do not realize that the seed is there until it germinates and the leaves break through the ground. Do you realize that by the time you see the leaves, the root system is already well established in the earth? The roots go down long before the leaves go up. We can have seeds of murder, hate, adultery, fornication, witchcraft, unforgiveness, idolatry, heresies, envy, lust, etc. By the time, we start seeing the manifestation of these things; they have already been rooted in our soul. After we notice the leaves, the manifestation of the seed, things only get worst.

I remember when I first bought my house in south Florida and my brother Everton came by and noticed that I had Florida willows growing in the yard. The trees were very small and few, and my brother explained that I needed to get them out as soon as possible, because they grow fast. Once they are established, it is hard to remove them. Well, I was too busy with other things going on in my life and failed to take heed to his advice. Florida willows do grow fast and spread even faster. Those little trees that look more like bushes turned into really big trees and they were growing everywhere. (When you cut the tree down it will spring back from the roots and are back to the same size in no time.) When we find things in our hearts that don't belong, we have to use the Word of God to identify them and uproot them as soon as possible. Any knowledge that rises up against the knowledge of God must be dealt with before it grows and gets out of hand.

Many years ago, I took my nephew and godson to the movies to watch the Incredible Hulk. While I was sitting there watching the movie and listening to the dialogue (eating the fruit), the Holy Spirit prompted me to pay attention to what I was watching and the hidden theme in the movie. I realized that the Incredible Hulk represented the spirit of anger, and the movie was actually getting children to believe if they give in to the spirit of anger, then it would make them strong and powerful. Anger was being glorified. I know some people will say it is just a movie, but you are wrong. I repeat, if people pay 5 million dollars for a 30-second Super Bowl commercial, knowing how that one commercial will influence people to buy their products by subliminal and not so subliminal messages, then what effect can a two-hour movie have on you and your children? After watching the movie, does a child embrace the anger when it comes, or do they fight it knowing anger can lead to death? **Many will still say they see no problem with it, but my question to you is, who are you going to believe, self or God's Word?**

Prov 22:24-25
24 Make no friendship with an angry man; and with a furious man thou shalt not go:
25 **Lest thou learn his ways, and get a snare to thy soul.**
KJV

Prov 29:22
22 An angry man stirreth up strife, and a furious man **aboundeth in transgression.** KJV

I have dealt with spirits of anger while doing deliverance on people in spiritual bondage. Some of them have taken on the appearance of scorpions, dangerous and poisonous. They are not easy to get out because many of the hosts (people that they are in) see them as helps. They believe the lies, from the demonic spirit feeding them, that anger makes them stronger. When they are angry, people leave them alone. When they are angry, they can control others. Yet the truth is that anger is a sure way to be entrapped by the devil to conclude with the death of yourself or others.

Movies that glorify anger are a way for anger demons to project themselves, and the corrupt knowledge of embracing rage, to the world. They identify victims who are enamored with the story of how anger can benefit them. When you spend two hours cheering an angry man and glorifying the demon of anger, then the proverb becomes confirmed in your life. You have befriended and idolized the angry man, many times unbeknown to you, and have learned his ways entrapping your own soul. Years later, you are sitting in prison because your anger has caused someone's death and you sit in the cell wondering, "How did I get here."

Millions of dollars are spent on movies to make them attractive to people. We call them action packed. The special effects are so striking that we can barely turn away. They make the fruit look sweet to us. It is like tasting a piece of pineapple and all you want to do after getting a taste is devour the whole thing. That movie trailer is the taste. They give you a taste of the story to draw you in. You come to get the whole fruit and consume it with the seed (hidden theme) that anger can make you powerful, and in the case of the Hulk, they are pushing the belief that you can be god-like. A small framed nerdy scientist becomes a violent weapon of destruction. In addition, after you watch the movie you go and tell all your friends how great it was and invite them to come see it also. Does this sound like what happened in the Garden?

The serpent came and showed Eve the movie trailer. It was her glimpse of what was showing in the theater. The trailer showed that man could become a god. Eve was captivated by the trailer and decided she was going to see the movie. She went to the theater (tree), ingested the sweet fruit of the movie, and the theme (seed) of being your own god was consumed also. She then went back to Adam with the same story (fruit) and he ingested. In the end, the trick of the devil and their own covetousness got them cursed and expelled from the garden.

Gen 3:4-6
4 And the serpent said unto the woman, Ye shall not surely die:
5 For God doth know that in **the day ye eat thereof, then your eyes shall be opened, and ye shall be as gods**, knowing good and evil.
6 And when the woman saw that the tree was good for food, and that it was pleasant to the eyes, and a tree to be desired to make one wise, she took of the fruit thereof, and did eat, and gave also unto her husband with her; and he did eat.
KJV

The devil has come a long way from the Garden, and although the fruit has been GMO'd it still carries part of the original DNA. It still comes down to ingesting the story with the hidden theme, which is the seed. People are the soil that the seed is planted in and they then become trees of death giving fruit to others, just as Eve gave the fruit to Adam.

I know many reading this are thinking I have never heard this before. Many have thought there was no way to know what the fruit was. Others have been told that it was a literal tree and fruit. There are even some of you who have been told that the fruit was sex (I will deal with that later). I love how God operates. Earlier in the book, I spoke on how God has a habit of hiding things in plain sight. This is not just in the Bible. Some of the things that God has hidden in plain sight are in nature. They show how He designed this universe and are amazing. God will also arrange things in the world to give evidence of His truth. I want you to take your hand and with your index finger reach up and place it right in the middle of your throat. What are you touching? Yes, it is your voice box from where your words originate. Yes! It is your ADAM'S APPLE! Adam's apple is the fruit, and those fruits are spoken words.

Chapter 4

As Trees

Mark 8:22-24
22 And he cometh to Bethsaida; and they bring a blind man
unto him, and besought him to touch him.
23 And he took the blind man by the hand, and led him out of
the town; and when he had spit on his eyes, and put his hands
upon him, he asked him if he saw ought.
24 And he looked up, and said, I see men as trees, walking.
KJV

I know what you are thinking. If the fruit was spoken words
then how could the tree be a tree? (SMILE) Cause I am smiling.
The tree is not a literal tree. Let's get it.

It is very important that I reiterate what was learned from the
earlier chapters. Please read this again:

Isa 28:9-10
9 **Whom shall he teach knowledge?** and **whom shall he make to
understand doctrine?** Them that are weaned from the milk, and
drawn from the breasts.
10 **For precept must be upon precept, precept upon precept;
line upon line, line upon line; here a little, and there a little:**
KJV

After the Holy Spirit gave me the revelation on the fruit, He
gave me a while to meditate on what He showed me. I was so

overjoyed with the fruit revelation that it took some time before I asked the logical question. If the fruit is not a fruit, then what is the tree? The understanding of the tree took a little longer. It was not a 15-minute run through the scriptures. The understanding of the tree is so powerful and branches off into many different areas. Each area opens up a plethora of knowledge.

I was reading Mark 8:22-24, and I asked myself a simple question. Why did Christ have to go through all that to heal the blind man? I mean He walked him outside the city, spit in his eyes, put His hands on him, and yet he still didn't see clearly. Finally, Christ touched his eyes and then he saw clearly.

Mark 8:25
25 After that he put his hands again upon his eyes, and made him look up: and he was restored, and saw every man clearly.
KJV

When you spend a lot of time in the Word of God, you start to get a feel of how God does things. **Anytime God takes you through a process when He or the Son are doing something, then there is hidden knowledge in what is being done.** All Christ had to do was say "be healed" as He has done on other occasions in scripture and the man would have been healed. He did it the way He did for a reason. Christ does not have to touch you twice to heal you. He was leaving us a clue of understanding. Let's look at another blind man that He healed.

John 9:6-7
6 When he had thus spoken, he **spat on the ground**, and made **clay of the spittle**, and **he anointed the eyes** of the blind man with the clay,
7 And said unto him, Go, **wash in the pool of Siloam, (which is by interpretation, Sent.)** He went his way therefore, and washed, and **came seeing.**
KJV

The interpretation of what Christ did is well known so I will not go into details. I will just give it. The spit represents the Word of God coming forth from the Father and mixing it with the clay is a metaphor for the Word of God mixing with flesh. That is Christ coming forth from the Father and becoming a man or putting on flesh. He anointed the man's eyes with the clay and spittle mix, which represents the blind unbeliever encountering Christ and believing. The blind man (believer) then goes to a pool named Sent, which represents the Holy Spirit that was sent from God. He goes into the pool, which represents us being baptized into the Body of Christ, and finally he came back seeing.

This healing is not the same process that Christ took with the first man. He was revealing something different. Christ does not have to touch you twice to heal you. He wanted the man to see the trees. It was all about the trees. Christ took him out of the town to get him away from the unbelievers. If Christ would have opened up his eyes to the spirit realm in town, Lord knows what he might have seen. When Christ took him apart from the town, the only ones there would have been the disciples and angels. Christ did not half heal the man as some teach; He gave him a glimpse into the spirit realm. He saw the trees that God had planted walking as men. Christ did this on purpose because it is a key to understanding what or who the trees in the Garden really are. With the blind man we have one man that saw both realms (spiritual and natural), but let's look at two men who saw one of each realm and do a comparison.

Angels at the river

Now I want to set this up for you. The Angel Gabriel has taken Daniel in a vision to the banks of the river. As he stands with him, Daniel describes what he is seeing. Please pay attention to the men and their location on the river:

Dan 12:5-7
5 Then I Daniel looked, and, behold, **there stood other two, the one on this side of the bank of the river,** and **the other on that side of the bank of the river.**
6 And one said to **the man clothed in linen, which was upon the waters of the river,** How long shall it be to the end of these wonders?
7 And I heard the man clothed in linen, **which was upon the waters of the river,** when he held up his right hand and his left hand unto

heaven, and sware by him that liveth for ever that it shall be for a time, times, and an half; and when he shall have accomplished to scatter the power of the holy people, all these things shall be finished. KJV

Daniel is seeing an angel (who appears as a man) on his side of the river, and he sees another angel on the other side of the river. There is also a third angel standing on the water in the middle of the river. Now I want to do a comparison with John who was also taken to a river in Revelation.

Rev 22:1-2
22:1 And he shewed me a **pure river of water of life**, clear as crystal, proceeding out of the throne of God and of the Lamb.
2 In the midst of the street of it, and on either side of the river, was there **the tree of life**, which bare twelve manner of fruits, and yielded her fruit every month: and the leaves of the tree were for the healing of the nations.
KJV

John saw a river of pure water coming from the throne of God. I told you before that God hides things in plain view. Over the years while ministering, I have asked many believers how many trees they see in those two verses. Very few people have seen the correct number. Let me explain what throws people off. You see that word "street" in verse two. It is not a street like a road. The Greek word translated street is *"plateia,"* it just means a wide-open space. The previous chapter is speaking about the city New Jerusalem. When people see the word street in this chapter their minds automatically sees it as a street in the city. I truly believe God planned it this way to hide the true meaning because Revelation is also a sealed (coded) book. If you read the beginning of verse two, carefully, you will see John is talking about an open space in the middle of the river. Rivers do not have streets. When I ask people how many trees of life John sees the majority say one, and some say two. The truth of the matter is there are three. One tree is in the open space in the middle of the river. One tree is on each side of the river (equaling two). The total adds up to three trees. Daniel and John are at the same river. Daniel saw angels and John saw trees of life. Yet the truth is, what they saw represent one and the same.

Now we understand why what Christ did with the blind man becomes so important because it brings the two together. **"Men as trees walking" is the catalyst to understand that men and angels are represented as trees in the Bible.** Let's go searching for some more pieces to the puzzle.

Ps 1:1-3
1:1 Blessed is the man that walketh not in the counsel of the ungodly, nor standeth in the way of sinners, nor sitteth in the seat of the scornful.
2 But his delight is in the law of the LORD; and in his law doth he meditate day and night.
3 And **he shall be like a tree planted by the rivers of water,** that bringeth forth **his fruit in his season;** his **leaf** also shall not wither; and whatsoever he doeth shall prosper.
KJV

Does verse three sound familiar? Fruit in season and leaves that do not wither are metaphors. Let's go back to revelation and do a comparison:

Rev 22:2
2 In the midst of the street of it, and on either side of the river, was there the **tree of life,** which bare **twelve manner of fruits, and yielded her fruit every month: and the leaves of the tree were for the healing of the nations.**
KJV

If you put a seed from the tree of life into some dirt (you are the dirt), and it grows up until it starts producing fruit, what type of tree does it become? Yes! We become trees of life. When we become trees of life, the Holy Spirit speaks life through us and we speak the correct thing at the correct time to facilitate life. The leaves represent our righteousness (through Christ) will not wither because we are planted by the river, which represents the Holy Spirit flowing.

Prov 11:30
30 **The fruit of the righteous is a tree of life;** and he that winneth souls is wise.
KJV

The righteous angels are trees of life. Righteous saints become trees of life. There is also a special tree of life, which sits in God's Garden and gives eternal life. Christ gave us the proper name for the Garden planted at the east of Eden and specified that those who overcome in this life will have access to this tree of life.

Rev 2:7
7 He that hath an ear, let him hear what the Spirit saith unto the churches; To him that overcometh will I give to eat of **the tree of life**, which is in the midst of **the paradise of God.**
KJV

Ok, let's reiterate what we have learned so far. We have learned that the Bible is a coded book in many sections. We have learned that it contains dark sayings and parables that we are able to understand by unraveling metaphors. We have learned that we have to put pieces of the puzzle together from different areas of the Bible with the help of the Holy Spirit. "Precept upon precept." We have learned that the fruit mentioned in the garden was spoken words that Eve embraced and shared with Adam who accepted them. We have learned that trees are a metaphor for angels and people. Ok!

We are not finished with the trees. We still have to identify the tree of death, which contains the knowledge of good and evil. I know a few writers have concluded that the tree is Satan but coming to a conclusion and proving it are two different things. I have never read of anyone proving it. LOL! I feel like a school kid in the back of the class raising my hand gleefully screaming me, me, me! LOL! When God fills you up, you just want to pour it out.

One of my favorite books in the Bible is Zechariah. I love the books that teach you the hidden meanings in other books. Job is my number one; Proverbs and Isaiah are up there too. Yet, we find in Zechariah another catalyst in understanding what took place in the Garden. Zechariah is taken up into a vision and shown by an angel some wondrous things in the spirit realm:

Zech 4:11-14

11 Then answered I, and said unto him, **What are these two olive trees upon the right side of the candlestick and upon the left side thereof?**

12 And I answered again, and said unto him, What be these two olive branches which through the two golden pipes empty the golden oil out of themselves?

13 And he answered me and said, Knowest thou not what these be? And I said, No, my lord.

14 Then said he, **These are the two anointed ones, that stand by the LORD of the whole earth.**

KJV

Zechariah is in heaven and observes two olive trees and a seven head lamp stand (Menorah). The angel asks him what he sees so right away we know knowledge is about to be released according to his observation. Zechariah asks the angel what are the two olive trees. The angel advises him that they are the two anointed ones that stand by the Lord of the whole earth. Many Christian scholars have taught that the olive trees represent Israel because Paul speaks of the olive tree in Rom 11 and he is definitely speaking about Israel. Remember I showed earlier that fruit is a metaphor with more than one meaning. Fruit of the womb (children), fruit of your doings (your actions), fruit of the lips (spoken words), etc. Well in the same way, the olive tree is a metaphor with more than one meaning. Yes, olive tree can stand for Israel, and it even stands for the two witnesses in Rev 11:4. Let's take a look at Revelations:

Rev 11:3-4

3 And I will give power unto my two witnesses, and they shall prophesy a thousand two hundred and threescore days, clothed in sackcloth.

4 **These are the two olive trees, AND the two candlesticks standing before the God of the earth.**

KJV

How can these two men be the two olive trees **and** the two candlesticks? They cannot. The two olive trees and the two candlesticks are operating through the two men who are prophets. The two candlesticks represent the seven Spirits of God. We have those seven Spirits operating through Israel in the Old Testament and then we see Christ going to heaven before the throne, and the angels say He is worthy to receive seven things:

Rev 5:12
12 Saying with a loud voice, Worthy is the Lamb that was slain to receive **power**, and **riches**, and **wisdom**, and **strength**, and **honour**, and **glory**, and **blessing**.
KJV

Saints, that is not just God showering things on Christ for the great work He did as the Lamb of God. These are the seven Spirits of God, identified by the seven areas they oversee. This is what the menorah seven-headed candlestick represents.

Sidenote: They are assigned by God, not by believers.

1. Angel over power*
2. Angel over riches*
3. Angel over wisdom*
4. Angel over strength*
5. Angel over honor
6. Angel over glory
7. Angel over blessings

We are talking about the Garden, so I cannot go deep into these things but maybe in a later book. I do want you to understand that these angels are **head angels** and have thousands if not more angels working under them. Christ is head over them all and this is what they were saying He was worthy to receive. I want to share one other thing on this subject before we get back to the tree. Read carefully:

Rev 5:13
13 And every creature which is in heaven, and on the earth, and under the earth, and such as are in the sea, and all that are in them, heard I saying, **Blessing**, and **honour**, and **glory**, and **power**, be unto him that sitteth upon the throne, and unto the Lamb for ever and ever.
KJV

Why is it that when addressing the Father and Lamb in the sense of eternity, they ascribe to them four things instead of seven? Why did they leave out riches, wisdom, and strength? Why is there a discrepancy with power? Do you know? Let me share this gem with you. The power given to Christ and the power attributed to the Lamb and the Father are two different Greek words. Christ receives "dunamis," and "kratos" is attributed to God and the Lamb. The word "kratos" actually means dominion. The four things attributed to God are what we give to Him willingly blessings, honor, glory, and dominion (of ourselves). What Christ receives is what God has for us. What Christ received is not for Him it is to be distributed to the people of God. God does not need our power, riches, wisdom, or strength. What is attributed to the Father and the Lamb "for ever and ever" is the only things we can give them.

Therefore, Christ received the seven Spirits of God, which was actually prophesied in the scriptures. **We are about to see once again why understanding metaphors in scripture is so important. Read this carefully:**

Zech 3:8-9
8 Hear now, O Joshua the high priest, thou, and thy fellows that sit before thee: for they are men wondered at: for, behold, I will bring forth **my servant the BRANCH.**
9 For behold **the stone** that I have laid before Joshua; upon **one stone shall be seven eyes**: behold, I will engrave the graving thereof, saith the LORD of hosts, and **I will remove the iniquity of that land in one day.**
KJV

Who is the **BRANCH**, and what is the stone with seven eyes?

Isa 11:1-5
Isaiah 11
11:1 And there shall come forth **a rod** out of **the stem of Jesse,** and **a Branch** shall grow out of his **roots:**
2 And the **spirit of the LORD** shall rest upon him, **the spirit of wisdom** and **understanding**, the **spirit of counsel** and **might**, the **spirit of knowledge** and of **the fear of the LORD;**

3 And shall make him of quick understanding in the fear of the LORD: and he shall not judge after the sight of his eyes, neither reprove after the hearing of his ears:

4 But with righteousness shall he judge the poor, and reprove with equity for the meek of the earth: and **he shall smite the earth with the rod of his mouth, and with the breath of his lips shall he slay the wicked.**

5 And righteousness shall be the girdle of his loins, and faithfulness the girdle of his reins.

KJV

This might not mean much to the average believer, but for those who really study the Bible and want to be exposed to the deeper things of God; this will be a powerful revelation. God in Isaiah 11:1 mentions Jesse and his name is combined with parts of a tree. It is nonsensical to the average reader but as I have said before, God hides things in plain sight. Pay attention because it is a riddle in the form of a puzzle.

You have a root, a stem (trunk), a rod, and a branch. All we need is one piece of the puzzle to figure out the whole thing and God gives us the piece. God says the stem (trunk) is Jesse. The stem of a tree sits on the roots. If Jesse is the stem (trunk) then who came before Jesse? Jesse's father name was Obed. Obed is the root. After the root (Obed) and stem (Jesse), we come to the rod. The rods are those big branches that come out of the trunk of a tree. We call them branches today but in actuality, they are rods. If you were going to make a rod that is the portion of the tree you would take to form the rod. Who comes after Jesse? I am hoping that every reader knows that Jesse is the father of King David. Therefore, David is the rod that comes out of the stem (trunk) of Jesse. Now we have the root as Obed, stem as Jesse, and rod as King David. Who is the branch, the outer most tip of the tree? Who is David's son? You got it, King Solomon. Let's look at verse 1 one more time.

Isa 11:1

11:1 And there shall come forth a rod out of the stem of Jesse, and **a Branch shall grow out of his roots:**

KJV

Trust me when I say only the Holy Spirit can reveal this. The writer under the inspiration of God is linking the branch to the root. That is why the two are placed last even though that is not how the tree is designed. Yet, there is something significant in the root and branch that identifies the **Him** that will have seven spirits resting on Him (verse 2). **The spirit of the Lord, spirit of wisdom, spirit of understanding, spirit of counsel, spirit of might, spirit of knowledge, and the spirit of the fear of the Lord.**

Did you notice earlier that wisdom possessed the same items as the branch?

Prov 8:12-14
12 **I wisdom** dwell with prudence, and find out **knowledge** of witty inventions.
13 **The fear of the LORD** is to hate evil: pride, and arrogancy, and the evil way, and the froward mouth, do I hate.
14 **Counsel** is mine, and sound **wisdom**: I am **understanding**; I have **strength**.
KJV

If you can understand the connection between the root and the branch, then you can understand who this person is. We all know it is Christ but as I said earlier, to know something and prove something can be two different things.

Branch = Solomon whose name means peace
Rod = David
Stem = Jesse
Root = Obed whose name means servant

What is the connection between Obed and Solomon (root and branch) that identifies the person in verse 2? Obed's name means servant and Solomon's name means peace. The servant is going to bring peace and specifically the gospel of peace. God wants us to know that the significance is in the names as later in the chapter He repeats that the root of Jesse (Obed/servant) is a sign:

Isa 11:10
10 And in that day there shall be **a root of Jesse**, which shall stand
for an ensign of the people; to it shall the Gentiles seek: and **his
rest shall be glorious.**
KJV

It is the servant of the Lord to whom all the gentiles will seek
and **He will bring rest (peace).**

Matt 11:28-29
28 Come unto me, all ye that labour and are heavy laden, and **I will
give you rest.**
29 Take my yoke upon you, and learn of me; for **I am meek and
lowly in heart: and ye shall find rest unto your souls.**
KJV

When Christ says that He is meek and lowly in heart, He
means that He has come as a servant. Christ came as the Lamb of
God to fulfill His Father's will and die as a servant for all those who
will believe. Now let us look back at Zechariah again:

Zech 3:8-9
8 Hear now, O Joshua the high priest, thou, and thy fellows that sit
before thee: for they are men wondered at: for, behold, I will bring
forth **my servant the BRANCH.**
9 For behold **the stone** that I have laid before Joshua; upon **one
stone shall be seven eyes**: behold, I will engrave the graving
thereof, saith the LORD of hosts, and **I will remove the iniquity of
that land in one day.**
KJV

Now I want to bring clarification on something. Christ did
not come to bring peace to the world. The world will not be in peace
until after judgment. **He came as the servant of the Father to
bring the Gospel of Peace to all those who believe.** There will be
no peace for the wicked.

John 14:27

27 **Peace I leave with you, my peace I give unto you**: not as the world giveth, give I unto you. Let not your heart be troubled, neither let it be afraid.
KJV

Luke 10:5-6

5 And into whatsoever house ye enter, first say, Peace be to this house.

6 And **if the son of peace be there, your peace shall rest upon it: if not, it shall turn to you again.**
KJV

Gospel of Peace

Isa 57:15-21

15 For thus saith the high and lofty One that inhabiteth eternity, whose name is Holy; I dwell in the high and holy place, **with him** also that is of a contrite and humble spirit, **to revive** the spirit of the humble, and to revive the heart of the contrite ones.

16 For I will not contend for ever, neither will I be always wroth: for the spirit should fail before me, and the souls which I have made.

17 **For the iniquity of his covetousness** was I wroth, and **smote him: I hid me**, and was wroth, and he went on frowardly in the way of his heart.

18 I have seen his ways, and **will heal him: I will lead him also, and restore comforts unto him and to his mourners.**

19 I create the fruit of the lips; **Peace, peace to him that is far off, and to him that is near, saith the LORD; and I will heal him.**

20 But the wicked are like the troubled sea, when it cannot rest, whose waters cast up mire and dirt.

21 **There is no peace, saith my God, to the wicked.**
KJV

For an in-depth study on the above verses and the Gospel of Peace, please see the books **"Assault on Innocence"** or the excerpt **"The Armor of God."**

Now that it has been affirmed that Christ is the servant called the branch and that He is the Wisdom spoken of in Prov 8, I want you to read the rest of Prov 8 so you can fully understand who Christ is. Please read slowly and carefully:

Prov 8:15-36

15 By me kings reign, and princes decree justice.

16 By me princes rule, and nobles, even all the judges of the earth.

17 **I love them that love me; and those that seek me early shall find me.**

18 Riches and honour are with me; yea, durable riches and righteousness.

19 **My fruit** is better than gold, yea, than fine gold; and my revenue than choice silver.

20 I lead in the way of righteousness, in the midst of the paths of judgment:

21 **That I may cause those that love me to inherit substance; and I will fill their treasures.**

22 **The LORD possessed me in the beginning of his way, before his works of old.**

23 **I was set up from everlasting, from the beginning, or ever the earth was.**

24 When there were no depths, **I was brought forth**; when there were no fountains abounding with water.

25 Before the mountains were settled, before the hills was **I brought forth:**

26 While as yet he had not made the earth, nor the fields, nor the highest part of the dust of the world.

27 When he prepared the heavens, I was there: when he set a compass upon the face of the depth:

28 When he established the clouds above: when he strengthened the fountains of the deep:

29 When he gave to the sea his decree, that the waters should not pass his commandment: when he appointed the foundations of the earth:

30 **Then I was by him, as one brought up with him**: and I was daily his delight, rejoicing always before him;

31 Rejoicing in **the habitable part of his earth**; and my delights were with the sons of men.

32 Now therefore hearken unto me, O ye children: for blessed are they that keep my ways.

33 Hear instruction, and be wise, and refuse it not.

34 **Blessed is the man that heareth me,** watching daily at my gates, waiting at the posts of my doors.

35 For **whoso findeth me findeth life, and shall obtain favour of the LORD.**

36 But **he that sinneth against me wrongeth his own soul: all they that hate me love death.**
KJV

If I had the space, I could take you through everything I highlighted and show where Christ confirms it. This is a powerful chapter and for those who have not figured it out, this is where John gets the understanding of who the Word of God is. The chapter above reveals that Christ was not created; He was brought forth, meaning He came out of the Father. The Father possessed Him before anything was. He repeats that He was brought forth just as the light was brought forth in the darkness. He said that He was set up from everlasting. He says He was always with the Father. He was in the habitable part of the earth (Garden). He said blessed is the man that heareth Me. Hear Him!

Mark 9:7

7 And there was a cloud that overshadowed them: and a voice came out of the cloud, saying, This is my beloved Son: **hear him.**
KJV

If you find Him you will find eternal life, yet those that hate Him love death. John knew the meaning of this chapter. He understood the mystery of the Kingdom and Christ's true identity:

John 1:1-5

1:1 In the beginning was the Word, and **the Word was with God, and the Word was God.**

2 The same was in the beginning with God.

3 **All things were made by him; and without him was not any thing made that was made.**

4 In him was life; and the life was the light of men.

5 And the light shineth in darkness; and the darkness comprehended it not.
KJV

Do you realize that as you are reading, you're picking up talents? Your knowledge of the mysteries of the Kingdom is increasing. Even as I write this book, I am receiving deeper understanding of what God has already deposited in me and He is adding more. We are trading because we are entwined in the things of God. When we trade in the things of God, we always leave with more than what we came with.

The Lord of the Whole Earth

Ok, let's get back on track in our discussion of the two olive trees. The key to understanding who or what the two olive trees are, that are seen by Zechariah, is understanding where they are located.

Zech 4:14
14 Then said he, **These are the two anointed ones, that stand by the LORD of the whole earth.**
KJV

The question is, do we have any scripture that gives us an indication of where the Lord of the whole earth is with two anointed ones standing next to Him? I have heard others quote Elijah, who often says in scripture that he stands before the Lord. They use his statement to justify saying that he is one of the anointed ones standing by the Lord. The only problem with this is that the scripture says that the two anointed ones stand BY the Lord of the whole earth and not BEFORE the Lord of the whole earth. An in-depth study also reveals that the Hebrew word used by Elijah for before is *paniym,* which indicates in front of one's face. Zechariah used the word *Al,* which indicates **next to and above**. God has always shown us where He resides on the earth and understanding the image He gave us is the key to understanding who the two olive trees are that stand by Him.

Ex 25:17-22
17 And thou shalt make a mercy seat of pure gold: two cubits and a half shall be the length thereof, and a cubit and a half the breadth thereof.
18 And thou shalt make **two cherubims of gold**, of beaten work shalt thou make them, in the two ends of the mercy seat.

19 And **make one cherub on the one end, and the other cherub on the other end: even of the mercy seat shall ye make the cherubims on the two ends** thereof.

20 And the cherubims shall stretch forth their wings on high, covering the mercy seat with their wings, and their faces shall look one to another; toward the mercy seat shall the faces of the cherubims be.

21 And thou shalt put the mercy seat above upon the ark; and in the ark thou shalt put the testimony that I shall give thee.

22 And there **I will meet with thee, and I will commune with thee from above the mercy seat, from between the two cherubims** which are upon the ark of the testimony, of all things which I will give thee in commandment unto the children of Israel.
KJV

God told Israel that He would dwell between the cherubims, and this is where He would meet with them. For those who might not know, cherubims are a type of angel. When God met with Abraham, before He destroyed Sodom, two men who are identified as angels accompanied him. These are the two olive trees. These are the two anointed ones. The image of the mercy seat with the two cherubim angels covering the area (where God would meet with man) with their wings symbolized an image in the natural of what is actually taking place in the spiritual. The angels are the covering of the Holy Place where God meets with men. They stand next to Him, and their wings are above Him covering Him.

Some might say, "But wait a minute. The scriptures say these are anointed ones. Men are anointed for God's purpose but not angels." Yet, that is not true; scripture shows angels are also anointed.

Ezek 28:14

14 **Thou art the anointed cherub that covereth**; and I have set thee so: thou wast upon the holy mountain of God; thou hast walked up and down in the midst of the stones of fire.
KJV

There is a great mystery tied into identifying these two cherubims that cover the mercy seat. Even the writer of the book of

Hebrews knew there was a mystery concerning the two angels. He was either not at liberty to reveal it or did not have the full understanding of it. Yet he mentioned it.

Heb 9:5

5 And over it the cherubims of glory shadowing the mercyseat; of which we cannot now speak particularly.
KJV

The mystery is not just tied into identifying the angels, it is also tied into what the mercy seat represents. This will be confirmed more in-depth in the upcoming chapters, but for now please take a little break and prepare your mind because we are about to go a whole   lot   deeper.

Chapter 5

The Tree Of Death Possessing Good And Evil

Please read slowly and carefully, noting that the King of Tyrus is Satan:

Ezek 28:12-19

12 Son of man, take up **a lamentation** upon the king of Tyrus, and say unto him, Thus saith the Lord GOD; **Thou sealest up the sum, full of wisdom, and perfect in beauty.**

13 Thou **hast been in Eden the garden of God**; every precious stone was thy covering, the sardius, topaz, and the diamond, the beryl, the onyx, and the jasper, the sapphire, the emerald, and the carbuncle, and gold: the workmanship of thy tabrets and of thy pipes was prepared in thee in the day that thou wast created.

14 **Thou art the anointed cherub that covereth**; and I have set thee so: thou wast upon the holy mountain of God; thou hast walked up and down in the midst of **the stones of fire**.

15 Thou wast perfect in thy ways from the day that thou wast created, till iniquity was found in thee.

16 By the multitude of thy merchandise they have filled the midst of thee with violence, and thou hast sinned: therefore **I will cast thee as profane out of the mountain of God: and I will destroy thee, O covering cherub**, from the midst of **the stones of fire**.

17 **Thine heart was lifted up because of thy beauty, thou hast corrupted thy wisdom by reason of thy brightness**: I will cast thee to the ground, I will lay thee before kings, that they may behold thee.

18 Thou hast defiled thy sanctuaries by the multitude of thine iniquities, by the iniquity of thy traffick; therefore will I bring forth a fire from the midst of thee, it shall devour thee, and I will bring thee to ashes upon the earth in the sight of all them that behold thee.
19 All they that know thee among the people shall be astonished at thee: thou shalt be a terror, and never shalt thou be any more.
KJV

If I were asked to give the simplest definition of the word lamentation, my response would be it is a sad funeral song. God instructs Ezekiel to pronounce a funeral song for the King of Tyrus. Tyrus is the ancient city Tyre, which was located in Phoenicia, north of Israel on the coast of what is now the Mediterranean. God gives the funeral song which would be considered beautiful poetry if it were not for the dire consequences being brought down on the king. We have to understand that the King of Tyrus is not the natural king of the city-state. In verse 13, God lets us know the person He is speaking of was in the Garden of Eden. Ezekiel is writing this around 580 bce, approximately 3,400 years after Adam and Eve were exiled from the Garden. More importantly, in verse 14 God shines a light on the fact that He is addressing a cherubim angel.

When God starts the funeral song, the first thing He notes is that this king/angel was **full of wisdom and perfect in beauty**. Please remember this; it will speak volumes a little later.

I know many people reading this have been taught that this was the serpent in the Garden. You have been told that the beautiful stones covered the body of the serpent. What I am going to show you is that God was not describing the serpent. He was describing the tree of death that contained the knowledge of Good and evil. The King of Tyrus was one of the two angels that stood next to the Lord of the whole earth. He was one of the covering cherubim angels as God states in verse 14.

Wisdom and Beauty

I want you to think about this: God zeros in on the fact that this cherubim angel that was in the Garden was wise and beautiful (verse 12). God then shows us that because of the reason of the angel's brightness, pride set in and he corrupted his wisdom. The beautiful and wise angel's wisdom became corrupted. Good mixed with evil. Let's take a little trip to the Garden, stand in Eve's shoes, and see what she saw:

Gen 3:6

6 And when the woman saw that **the tree** was good for food, and that it was **pleasant to the eyes**, and a tree to be **desired to make one wise**, she took of the fruit thereof, and did eat, and gave unto her husband with her; and he did eat.
KJV

Two things stand out when Eve went to the tree. The tree was **beautiful** (pleasant to the eyes) and the tree was **full of wisdom** (desired to make one wise). God mentions these same two attributes of the cherubim angel that covered. **Ladies and gentlemen, the tree was Satan himself.** The tree was the tree that stands next to the Lord of the whole earth. The tree was the cherubim angel. Now we understand what Satan was doing in the Garden. The Garden of paradise was a place created by God where He would meet with mankind. Adam the first man (as stated in scripture) was in charge of keeping the place.

If you pay close attention to the scripture about the two trees in the midst of the Garden, you will see by the wording of the scripture that the two trees in the midst were separate from the rest of the trees.

Gen 2:9

9 And out of the ground made the LORD God to grow every tree that is pleasant to the sight, and good for food; **the tree of life also in the midst of the garden, and the tree of knowledge of good and evil.** KJV

The two trees in the midst had a special purpose that went beyond the other trees located in the Garden. They were not trees; they were two angels that were placed in the Holy Space in the midst of the Garden, where God met with Adam. **Adam had the permission of God to speak to one but not the other who was Satan.**

God knew what was inside Satan, so He told Adam not to go and speak to him (eat from the tree). Remember, He told Adam first, not Eve. The same corrupt knowledge that was bubbling up inside Satan is the fruit of his lips that Eve took and ate and then went and fed to her husband Adam.

I want to reiterate that I understand that many people reading this book were taught that the fruit was a sex thing but I will show you that could not be it. How could eating the fruit be sex when God already told them they could eat from any of the trees (to include the tree of life)? God was not telling Adam to go and have sex with the other trees to include the tree of life. See how easily false doctrine is exposed when we do not look past the obvious. **It was spoken knowledge that was corrupt, Eve ingested it, and Adam did also.** It was never about sex; it was always about spoken knowledge, as scripture confirms. It was about making a choice between true wisdom and corrupt wisdom, and Adam and Eve made the wrong choice. They chose spiritual death over life. They had the choice to eat from (listen to) the other angel (tree of life) who had pure uncorrupted wisdom. They chose to eat from Satan instead.

Prov 3:13-18
13 **Happy is the man that findeth wisdom,** and **the man that getteth understanding.**
14 For the merchandise of it is better than the merchandise of silver, and the gain thereof than fine gold.
15 She is more precious than rubies: and all the things thou canst desire are not to be compared unto her.
16 **Length of days is in her right hand; and in her left hand riches and honour.**
17 Her ways are ways of pleasantness, and all her paths are peace.
18 **She is a tree of life to them that lay hold upon her:** and happy is every one that retaineth her.
KJV

The covering stones

Now that we have established who the tree was, let's close up some loose ends. As I said earlier, there are many teachings in the modern Christian church about the serpent (some we will deal with in the next chapter) and the stones that God mentioned in Ezekiel 28. One teaching is that the serpent's body was covered with precious stones. One would say, how could it be the tree that God was talking about since no one has seen a tree covered with gems? My answer to that is how many gem-covered snakes have you seen roaming around? The stones are not a physical covering because nowhere in scripture do we see any angel described as having a body covered with gems. However, we do have a symbolic figure covered not just with gems but the very same gems mentioned by Ezekiel, as possessed by the serpent, plus three more:

Ezek 28:13

13 Thou hast been in Eden the garden of God; every precious stone was thy covering, **the sardius, topaz, and the diamond, the beryl, the onyx, and the jasper, the sapphire, the emerald, and the carbuncle, and gold:** the workmanship of thy tabrets and of thy pipes was prepared in thee in the day that thou wast created. KJV

Ex 28:15-22

15 And thou shalt make **the breastplate of judgment** with cunning work; after the work of the ephod thou shalt make it; **of gold,** of blue, and of purple, and of scarlet, and of fine twined linen, shalt thou make it.

16 Foursquare it shall be being doubled; a span shall be the length thereof, and a span shall be the breadth thereof.

17 And thou shalt set in it settings of stones, even four rows of stones: the first row shall be **a sardius, a topaz, and a carbuncle:** this shall be the first row.

18 And the second row shall be **an emerald, a sapphire, and a diamond.**

19 And the third row **a ligure, an agate, and an amethyst**.

20 And the fourth row **a beryl, and an onyx, and a jasper:** they shall be set in gold in their inclosings.

21 And **the stones shall be with the names of the children of Israel**, twelve, according to their names, like the engravings of a signet; every one with his name shall they be according to the twelve tribes.

22 And thou shalt make upon the breastplate chains at the ends of wreathen work of pure gold. KJV

Each stone on the breastplate of the High Priest represented one of the tribes of Israel, and the High Priest had authority given by God to issue judgment over the tribes. If you do a study on the breastplate you will also find out that it is called the breastplate of judgment, righteousness, and faith/love. You need to be operating in faith and love, which together equals righteousness and then you have authority to judge righteously.

God said that Satan walked among the stones of fire, which in scriptures are a metaphor for angels. This indicates that he had authority over other angels and the gems represented the different groups. The high priest wore 12 gems set in gold. Satan had nine set in gold. Who were the nine groups he had authority over? I do not believe we will know this until we set foot in the Kingdom or God releases the revelation.

Satan was created perfect with his own free will. He allowed his brilliance to corrupt his wisdom. God said he sinned. Iniquity was found in him. He had so much, in beauty and wisdom. He possessed great authority, but he let it get to his head and God was letting him and all the world know he would be cast as profane out of heaven and will meet destruction in his final judgment.

Sidenote: I know many have taught that Satan was the worship leader in heaven and that the tabrets and pipes mentioned in verse 13 justify this conclusion. I cannot support this teaching and scripture does not either. Even though tabret (tambourine) is mentioned, the Hebrew word translated "pipes" in the verse is "*neqeb*," which is a bezel, a rim where you would place a jewel. I believe many of the translations say pipes because tabrets are often mentioned in scripture with pipes like a flute but it is an entirely different Hebrew word used "*chaliyl.*" If someone has received a personal revelation of Satan being heavens worship leader, I will not speak against it other than to say this interpretation is not supported in scripture. **If scripture does not support something, then it is just a conjecture coming from a private interpretation of the revealer.**

Chapter 6

Seraphims And Snakes

2 Cor 11:14
14 And no marvel; for Satan himself is transformed into an angel of light.
KJV

Over the years, I have had the opportunity to witness to quite a few atheists. I have often heard the line, "You don't expect me to believe a book with talking snakes?" I use this as an opportunity to explain to them that the serpent in the Garden was not a snake and share the deeper understanding of the true identity of the serpent. Normally when I am finished, there is a period of silence. I can feel that their foundation of understanding of the Bible has been shaken. I can tell that they are worried because if what I just told them can make so much sense, then (they are thinking) maybe the Bible just might be the truth.

I promise you that after you hear the truth about the serpent, it is going to be a powerful weapon to counteract the unbelief in people you know. It will make them stop and think.

I kept coming across this same scripture, 2 Cor 11: 14, where Paul is speaking about Satan transforming into an angel of light. I kept finding myself asking the same question, "When?" As a teacher in the Body of Christ, I have read the Bible hundreds of times. I know there are certain scriptures that I have read thousands of times. Yet I have never come to a place where Satan transformed into an angel of light. At least I thought I did not. It puzzled me to the point of asking God for clarification on it. I did not get an immediate response, so I started trying to consider the different possibilities. I left with two that were credible. Either Paul had received it as a revelation from God that he never wrote in an epistle, or somewhere in scripture it was hidden. **Knowing God, it was probably hidden in plain view. I then remembered what the Holy Spirit had shown me. Every puzzle, riddle, or mystery in scripture has to be solved by scripture and not something we come up with on our own.** You do not get an answer for Biblical mysteries from an outside source; it has to come from scriptures. I was left with only one conclusion. What Paul was talking about was in scripture and I needed to find it. Thank God for the Holy Spirit.

1 Cor 2:9-12
9 But as it is written, Eye hath not seen, nor ear heard, neither have entered into the heart of man, the things which God hath prepared for them that love him.
10 But **God hath revealed them unto us by his Spirit: for the Spirit searcheth all things, yea, the deep things of God.**
11 For what man knoweth the things of a man, save the spirit of man which is in him? even so the things of God knoweth no man, but the Spirit of God.
12 Now we have received, not the spirit of the world, but the spirit which is of God; **that we might know the things that are freely given to us of God.**
KJV

Wisdom is freely given to us:

James 1:5-6
5 **If any of you lack wisdom, let him ask of God, that giveth to all men liberally, and upbraideth not; and it shall be given him.**
6 But let him ask in faith, nothing wavering. For he that wavereth is like a wave of the sea driven with the wind and tossed.
KJV

Position yourself in right standing with God and ask Him, then open your Bible and search. The Holy Spirit will reward your effort by leading you to the right places. Sometimes it will be a quick answer and other times it may take a while. The situation is helped according to what you already know and how much time you spend in the scriptures. Some things learned of God must have the foundation laid first before God builds on it. Therefore, there might be some delay until you are mature enough to receive the revelation in what you requested, but He will answer you.

I started breaking down the scripture (2 Cor 11:14) and realized something. They did not have any light bulbs!

LOL! If you could see the look on your face. LOL! Paul never saw a light bulb with all its white shining light. When Paul speaks about an angel of light, what type of light was he talking about? He never saw a light bulb. When we speak about light, we picture white light because it is what we are used to seeing. In ancient times when they talked about turning on the light, they were talking about the light of a candle, which looks nothing like a light bulb. I went into the Greek to see the Greek meaning for the word translated "light." The Greek word he used was **"*Phos*."** The meaning of the word is "to shine" but I remember how I was surprised at how many revelations I had received about angels that looked like flames of fire. The burning bush was an angel. The Bible also speaks about angels whose bodies appeared like fire. Other angels were balls of fire. I started thinking maybe I was onto something and went on an expedition for understanding:

Ex 3:2
2 And **the angel of the LORD appeared unto him in a flame of fire** out of the midst of a bush: and he looked, and, behold, the bush burned with fire, and the bush was not consumed.
KJV

Ezek 1:13
13 As for the likeness of the living creatures, **their appearance was like burning coals of fire, and like the appearance of lamps**: it went up and down among the living creatures; and **the fire was bright, and out of the fire went forth lightning.**
KJV

Now I started noticing there were quite a few places in scripture where ministering angels appeared as flames of fire. In addition, as I looked back at the scripture, Paul speaks of Satan as an angel of light. I took a closer look at the next verse and realized Paul was speaking about Satan appearing as a ministering angel.

2 Cor 11:14-15
14 And no marvel; for Satan himself is transformed into an angel of light.
15 Therefore it is no great thing if **his ministers** also **be transformed as the ministers of righteousness;** whose end shall be according to their works.
KJV

Read carefully:

Ps 104:4
4 Who maketh his angels spirits; **his ministers a flaming fire**:
KJV

Paul was using Satan as an example of his ministers pretending to be ministers of righteousness because Satan had appeared as a ministering angel, which according to scripture takes on the semblance of a flame of fire (angel of light). Some might think, "Well, why didn't Paul just say fire?" Actually **PHOS** is translated fire in scripture (Mark 14:54), but as I said before, God likes to hide things in plain sight. Now I understood that the Holy Spirit was taking me somewhere, I just did not know where we were going. I do not know how I ended up at Numbers 21:6, but I was there reading about the fiery serpents. I have never seen one of them and the concept was interesting, but I was in for the shock of my life when I went into the Hebrew manuscript to see if I could get a better understanding. SERAPH! It literally said God sent seraphim serpents to bite the people. Now this is the exact same word used in Isaiah 6, which leaves little wiggle room in the identification of what they were:

Isa 6:2-3

2 Above it stood **the seraphims**: each one had six wings; with twain he covered his face, and with twain he covered his feet, and with twain he did fly.

3 And one cried unto another, and said, Holy, holy, holy, is the LORD of hosts: the whole earth is full of his glory.

KJV

I remember as a young Christian lying on my bed one night, and God took me into a vision where the roof of the room was removed and I could see into the night sky. Directly above me, high in the sky, I saw a snake that had wings circling above. It was just flying around in a circle. It made no negative actions towards me but I remember I was weary of its presence. I knew God did not send it, and it was definitely keeping an eye on me. I cannot remember the details of the purpose for God showing me this, but I will always remember the vision because I thought the snake looked weird with the two wings. Over the years, God has shown me many things in the spirit realm, which has given me the understanding of the vastness of shapes, sizes, and forms of spiritual entities. Folks, there are many things out there that we have little understanding of.

We, who abide in the natural realm, often conclude that things of the spirit realm take on the appearance of things in the natural realm. My experience has shown me this is not necessarily true. Angels are not formed to look like men. Men are formed after the semblance of the image of God and angels are also. The four living creatures that stand by God's throne with the four faces of an eagle, lion, man, and ox are not made to look like creatures of this world. Creatures of this world were made to look like them.

Why am I saying this? It is to prepare your mind for what the Holy Spirit and scripture revealed about the seraphims. Some of them either look like or take on the form of snakes:

Num 21:5-9

5 And the people spake against God, and against Moses, Wherefore have ye brought us up out of Egypt to die in the wilderness? For there is no bread, neither is there any water; and our soul loatheth this light bread.

6 And the LORD sent **fiery serpents** among the people, and they bit the people; and much people of Israel died.

7 Therefore the people came to Moses, and said, We have sinned, for we have spoken against the LORD, and against thee; pray unto the LORD, that he take away **the serpents** from us. And Moses prayed for the people.

8 And the LORD said unto Moses, Make thee **a fiery serpent**, and set it upon a pole: and it shall come to pass, that every one that is bitten, when he looketh upon it, shall live.

9 And Moses made **a serpent** of brass, and put it upon a pole, and it came to pass, that if **a serpent** had bitten any man, when he beheld **the serpent** of brass, he lived.

KJV

The scripture is pretty clear-cut. The people spoke against God and Moses. God sent serpents among them. When the serpents bit them, the people died. The people cried out to Moses. Moses prayed for the people. God told Moses to make an image of an angel and set it on a pole that when the people who looked on it, had been bitten, they would be healed. Moses made an image on a pole of a snake and it worked.

Hold on! Wait a minute! "God told Moses to make an image of an angel?" What?! Yes, God told Moses in the Hebrew manuscript to make an image of a seraph (angel), not a snake. When Moses made the image of the seraphim, guess what it looked like? It looked just like a snake. The Hebrew word for snake is *"nachash,"* which is translated serpent but means a snake. If we were to go back through the verses with the Hebrew understanding, then it would read something like this: The people acted a fool. God sent seraphim (angel) serpents among them. When the serpents (nachash) bit them, the people died. The people cried out to Moses. Moses prayed for the people. God told Moses to make an image of an angel (seraphim) and set it on a pole that when the people which looked on it, had been bitten, they would be healed. Moses made an image on a pole of a snake (nachash) and it worked.

Why does the scripture say God sent seraphim snakes? Why did God tell Moses to make an image of a seraphim? Scholars have tried to explain this by saying God called the snakes seraphims, because they were copper in color, so He was alluding to their fiery appearance. Others have stated that the snakes' bite caused a burning in their victims and the word seraph could indicate the burning feeling. Lastly, some scholars say because they move so fast when they strike God used the word seraph with nacash (snake) to show this. All of this is plausible but there is no direct scriptural support. There are many scriptures where the venom and poison of asps and vipers are spoken about and the word seraphim is nowhere in sight. Other scriptures use words for viper or asp that are also fast striking snakes, yet they are not combined with seraph. In ancient Hebrew, you have three similar words. Sar' aph (sar-af) meaning a thought, saraph (saw-raf) which means burning, and saraph (saw-rawf) meaning a fiery or saraph angel.

Now I want you to read this verse carefully:

Isa 14:29
29 Rejoice not thou, whole Palestina, because the rod of him that smote thee is broken: for out of the **serpent's** root shall come forth a **cockatrice**, and his fruit shall be a **fiery flying serpent**.
KJV

Now these are the three Hebrew words used for the three types of snakes in the verse in the order of placement. Nachash (serpent), Tsepha (cockatrice), saraph (fiery flying serpent).

There are only two credible conclusions that we can come to from the scriptural evidence. Either seraphim angels have the ability to take on the form of a snake and that is why God called them seraphs in the book of Numbers, or there is a type of snake that resembles seraphim angels in color or form. Either way, it still confirms that seraphs are linked to serpents in some way. Christ Himself collaborates on the connection between serpents and angels (fallen):

Luke 10:19-20
19 Behold, I give unto you power to tread on **serpents and scorpions**, and over all **the power of the enemy**: and nothing shall by any means hurt you.

20 Notwithstanding in this rejoice not, that **the spirits are subject unto you**; but rather rejoice, because your names are written in heaven.
KJV

The scripture clearly shows that the spirits, which are the enemy that Christ gave them power over, are the serpents and scorpions. These are the enemy that we fight against daily. These are fallen angels, the forces of evil.

I have said all this to get you to understand that the serpent in the Garden was not a snake, but was Satan himself disguised as a seraphim angel. He is called a serpent as a metaphorical dark saying to hide the mystery of what took place in the Garden until it was time to be revealed. Satan was the tree, which has already been shown was a cherub angel. He took on the form of a ministering angel, a seraph, when he went to talk to Eve. He needed to deceive her into coming to the tree of the knowledge of good and evil, which was himself. He transformed into a ministering angel because Eve was used to them. They are the ones that facilitated messages from God.

When Paul, who noted Satan transformed into a seraphim angel, stated that Eve was deceived, he was not just talking about the conversation. The deception was also in Satan's appearance as a messenger angel. He utilized a form she would be open to receive. The deception worked. Many will ask why God allowed it. God does not test us with evil but He does allow the test of our faith so we know what is in us. He allowed Eve and Adam to be tested to reveal to them their faith. In the same way, God allowed the Gibeonites to test Israel on His commandments about the people of the land. This is the same way He is testing believers today to show us our faith in Him and His promises. It has always been God's way.

Surely

While teaching a study group, the Holy Spirit showed me how crafty, the devil was in his attack on the faith of Eve. I was lead to hold up a blue plastic cup right in the face of each individual and ask them to examine the cup. Once they were satisfied with their examination, I put the cup to the side out of their view and asked what color was the cup? They would all say blue. I then asked if they were sure, and shockingly every single person would turn to where I had placed the cup to make sure it was blue. Even though they had clearly seen the color, by me interjecting the word "sure" it created a sliver of doubt. The doubt manifested causing them to turn to look at a cup they should have been certain was blue. A word of doubt interjected by the enemy can take us away from living by faith, which is believing in God's promises, to living by sight, which is to trust in self.

2 Cor 5:7
7(For we walk by faith, not by sight :)
KJV

God knew where Adam and Eve's faith was and that is why He instructed them not to have dialogue with the devil the covering cherub (tree of death). **God told them he was dangerous to them and that his words (fruit) would cause them spiritual death.** He would convince them not to trust God. Sadly, I see this same trick of the devil in play almost every day in the world. People are still falling for the same old trick. Two words were enough to shake the foundation of Eve's faith.

Gen 3:2-6
2 And the woman said unto the serpent, We may eat of the fruit of the trees of the garden:
3 But of the fruit of the tree which is in the midst of the garden, God hath said, Ye shall not eat of it, neither shall ye touch it, lest ye die.
4 And the serpent said unto the woman, Ye shall **not surely** die:
5 For **God doth know** that in the day ye eat thereof, **then your eyes shall be opened, and ye shall be as gods**, knowing good and evil.
6 And when the woman saw that the tree was good for food, and that it was pleasant to the eyes, and a tree to be desired to make one wise, she took of the fruit thereof, and did eat, and gave also unto her husband with her; and he did eat.
KJV

The NOT SURELY was enough to cast doubt in Eve's mind. She turned to look back at the blue cup. The devil came in for the kill. While her eyes were off the word of God and its truth, he came in with the knock out blow. He made her feel as if God was keeping something from her. God does not want you to be a god. He is holding you back. He does not want you to be like Him. When your faith is already shaken, the lies drop as sledgehammers against your shield of faith that has already started to crack. Her wall of defense, which is trusting in God, crumbled and she was led to the slaughter.

Heb 10:38-39
38 Now the just shall live by faith: but if any man draw back, my soul shall have no pleasure in him.
39 But we are not of them who draw back unto perdition; but of them that believe to the saving of the soul.
KJV

Think about this question. Why did the devil attack Eve and not Adam? No! Really, stop and think about it. I will wait right here for you.

See, I told you I would wait right here for you.

Eve's faith was built on second hand promises. God never told her not to eat from the tree, He told Adam. When God instructed Adam about not eating from the tree, Eve was still a rib.

Gen 2:16-17
16 And the LORD God commanded **the man**, saying, Of every tree of the garden thou mayest freely eat:
17 But **of the tree of the knowledge of good and evil, thou shalt not eat of it: for in the day that thou eatest thereof thou shalt surely die.**
KJV

God warned me after He anointed me as a teacher in the Body of Christ that I am not to be a middleman between believers and Christ. My job is to introduced, them to Him, and let them develop a relationship with Him. I am not to be a go-to between Him and them. Each believer has to develop a personal relationship with Christ and the Father. Even Christ as the mediator between the

Father and men commanded us to pray to the Father in His name because He wants us to realize we have access to the Father.

Earlier, I said that understanding the mysteries of God's Kingdom allows us to learn lessons that take us from faith to love and everything in between. Here is an example. The devil realized that Eve got the commandment from Adam secondhand, so there was room to create doubt in her heart because she did not get her info from the source. Find me a Christian that does not read the Bible but relies on the word he receives from others and I will show you a Christian easily shaken. In the same way when the enemy is attacking a church or group, those that have not had personal experiences with God are the first to fall away. They are the easiest targets. These are the people that need others to pray for them because they have never developed a strong prayer life with answered prayers for themselves. These are those who have not experienced God's miraculous work in their lives. **When you know God on a personal level through experiencing Him, it is very hard to attack your faith.**

When I am ministering to new converts, I always focus first on them receiving the baptism of the Holy Spirit and insuring they pray correctly to get answered prayers. Once they have that connection through His Spirit and see Him working in answering their prayers, they are experiencing God. They know Him. Those who do not know Him are in for a lot of trouble in their Christian walk and are easily pulled away by the world. This is not new:

Judg 2:10-11
10 And also all that generation were gathered unto their fathers: and there arose another generation after them, **which knew not the LORD, nor yet the works which he had done for Israel.**
11 And the children of Israel did evil in the sight of the LORD, and served Baalim:
KJV

When the generation arose in Israel that had not experienced the miracles of God as He led them out of Egypt, they were pulled away into idol worship. Yes, they were told of all God did by their parents but it was secondhand information. They never experienced God.

In like manner, Eve's faith was built on secondhand information and was the easier target in an attack. We know this because she said she was not to touch the tree, which is not accurate of what God told Adam. Somebody ad-libbed. Is it an excuse for her sin? No, it is not but it gives us insight into how the enemy of our souls plots. He looks for the weak first and at the top of his list are those who have not experienced God or their faith is based on secondhand information.

Sidenote: I want to encourage those that have not been able to see God for who He is because your view is blocked by an apostle, bishop, pastor, etc. Ministers in the Body are just vessels utilized to bring about God's will. We follow God always and not the vessel. The vessel brings the living waters, but if we follow the vessel, we will end up at a factory full of empty vessels. If we follow the Living Waters that the vessel brings we will end up at the fountain in the throne room, which is the source of the Living Waters. God is not a respecter of persons. He draws close to all those who draw close to Him. If you want to experience God, then seek Him because He promises that those who seek Him diligently will find Him. **Yet as believers, we must understand that when we meet Him, it will be on His terms, not ours.** Why is it that some Christians have had so many experiences with God and yet others have none? Those that experience God on a consistent basis understand we meet God on His terms not on ours. Christ blood gives us access to the Holy of Holies but we cannot enter any kind of way.

James 4:8
8 Draw nigh to God, and he will draw nigh to you. Cleanse your hands, ye sinners; and purify your hearts, ye double minded.
KJV

Adam's Sin

Ask yourself this question: What was Adam's sin? Many will look at the situation and say Adam's sin was disobedience. Yes, he disobeyed God and that was the problem, but what was the issue that caused it? The secret is in the fruit. What did Satan present as the bait? Let's reiterate the trailer scenario. The fruit is a movie and the theme of the movie is the seed. The serpent presented the trailer for the movie to Eve to entice her. The trailer spoken by the serpent got her attention and Eve went and watched the whole movie (dialogue with Satan). She then took everything she learned from the movie and replayed it for Adam. He sat and watched (ingested) instead of rebuking her. Eve ate the fruit and the seed gestated and grew within her. The seed grew into a tree within her and then finally produced fruit, which Adam ate. Trailers are normally the best part of the movie used to draw people to see it. If we examine the trailer (what the serpent said) then we can identify Adams's sin:

Gen 3:4-5
4 And the serpent said unto the woman, Ye shall not surely die:
5 For God doth know that in the day ye eat thereof, then your eyes shall be opened, **and ye shall be as gods**, knowing good and evil.
KJV

Everybody wants to be a superhero. Everybody wants to be more than God made him or her to be. Men covet (wrongfully desire) to be like a god. When we do that, we are telling God He got it wrong and we deserve more. If He allowed, we would not stop wanting more until we wanted His position. We would not be satisfied until like Satan, we would want to be God Himself. Scripture confirms that Adam's sin was covetousness:

Isa 57:17
17 For **the iniquity of his covetousness** was I wroth, and smote him: I hid me, and was wroth, and he went on frowardly in the way of his heart.
KJV

Have you noticed how many entertainers and athletes are shown in the media as super men or even gods? Women entertainers are called divas, which is a term from the Hindu religion for gods. The very term idol, which comes from the Bible, refers to gods. Stars in the Bible are angels and when you become a superstar you are more than an angel, you're a god. Men are given acronyms like G.O.A.T. meaning the greatest of all times. We see people who confess to being Christians giving worship to entertainers who have taken names like Hova and Yeezus in direct blaspheme of the Father and Son. Yet some naive Christians will be at their concerts cheering them, which is a form of worship not understanding that these people are blaspheming the Godhead. These people want worship and they are not satisfied with being called kings and queens, they want to go to the next level to be called gods. The deceived of the world are too often ready to oblige. I read a meme on Facebook that asked the question, "How are you a god with a doctor's appointment?" Men and women are falling for the same lie from the Garden wanting to be gods and selling their souls for a worthless title. Then they end up in crisis hospitals, drug treatment facilities, or the grave because they are fake gods that cannot escape out of human situations.

It seems that covetous mentality has been passed down over the ages throughout the entire world. No one is satisfied with who they are or what they have. Everyone wants more and more and more. Think about it. Adam had dominion over everything in the natural world. He had a beautiful wife, peace, and everything he needed to be happy. Yet he wanted more. It reminds me today of when we see millionaires and billionaires still working hard to get more, not realizing they have all they need. They waste their lives acquiring more and more of "the stuff" and as they get closer to death, they realize it is worthless.

The natural will not transform with you into the spiritual. You cannot convert the money, houses, and things. What you know of God and His Kingdom will be all you are taking with you. Christ warns us to be wise and seek the Kingdom, and not the things of this life:

Luke 12:15
15 And he said unto them, Take heed, and **beware of covetousness**: for a man's life consisteth not in the abundance of the things which he possesseth.
KJV

I want you to take your time in reading these verses. This is a powerful warning of which all believers need to take heed:

Luke 12:16-21

16 And **he spake a parable unto them**, saying, The ground of a certain rich man brought forth plentifully:

17 And he thought within himself, saying, What shall I do, because I have no room where to bestow my fruits?

18 And he said, This will I do: I will pull down my barns, and build greater; and there will I bestow all my fruits and my goods.

19 And I will say to my soul, Soul, thou hast much goods laid up for many years; take thine ease, eat, drink, and be merry.

20 But **God said unto him, Thou fool, this night thy soul shall be required of thee: then whose shall those things be, which thou hast provided?**

21 So is he that layeth up **treasure for himself, and is not rich toward God.**

KJV

The more you know and apply the things of God and His Kingdom, the richer you are in this world and the world to come. **It is not about the abundance of things; it is wealth in the knowledge of God.**

Therefore, the devil used worthless knowledge to entrap Adam in his own covetousness. Adam had it all and did not realize it. In the end, he lost his position, home, dominion, and relationship with God chasing after what he could never have.

Many will ask, "If God knew the devil had become corrupt, then why did He still have him in his position?" We have to realize that we do not see or experience time in the same way that God does. Remember:

Ps 90:4

4 For **a thousand years in thy sight are but as yesterday** when it is past, and as a watch in the night.

KJV

2 Peter 3:8

8 But, beloved, be not ignorant of this one thing, that **one day is with the Lord as a thousand years, and a thousand years as one day.** KJV

In God's eyes, it has only been 6 days since the devil became corrupt, and 2 and a half days since he passed judgment on him. Satan's end is coming swift and sure. It only seems like a long time to us who are limited in natural bodies that are like vapor.

James 4:14

14 Whereas ye know not what shall be on the morrow. For what is your life? **It is even a vapour, that appeareth for a little time, and then vanisheth away.**

KJV

Hidden in the garden

The most beautiful and wise cherubim angel that was assigned as the covering angel for the Lord of the whole earth was lifted up in pride because of his status, wisdom, and beauty. God recognized this and saw that he had become corrupt. God warned Adam and Eve not to go around him because the corrupt mindset that he possessed would corrupt their minds. Satan with wicked intentions and realizing God had warned man to stay away from him disguised himself as a messenger angel (seraphim) and went to Eve to deceive her. He put on the form of a ministering angel of fire like the one who spoke to Moses in the burning bush and talked her into going and talking to the cherubim angel, which was himself. Eve went to Satan in his real form as the covering cherub angel (tree of knowledge of good and evil), the tree of death, and ingested his poisonous words (fruit). What Satan told Eve, she took and shared with Adam who ingested it also, as can be seen by his change of behavior. You can't hide from God.

Chapter 7

In The Cool Of The Day

Gen 3:8
8 And they heard **the voice** of the LORD God walking in the garden in the **cool of the day**: and Adam and his wife hid themselves from the presence of the LORD God amongst the trees of the garden.
KJV

Now here goes Christ walking in the Garden. What? Oh, you didn't know that it was Christ and not the Father walking in the Garden all those times with Adam? My bad! Let me break down the understanding for you. When the Bible was translated from Hebrew (sometimes through other languages) to English, the scholars came across a problem. In verse 8, they translated the Hebrew words *"ruwach yowm"* to cool of the day because the real meaning made no sense. Ruwach means spirit and yowm means day but spirit of the day made no sense. Probably, one of the scholars thought that Moses (the writer) must have meant that they were walking in the evening time when the cool winds blow. This is the only place throughout the scriptures where ruwach is translated cool. Almost everywhere else, it is translated spirit, which is the actual meaning.

I have a feeling I know how they came up with cool of the day. Read this:

John 3:8
8 The **wind bloweth** where it listeth, and thou hearest the sound thereof, but canst not tell whence it cometh, and whither it goeth: so is every one that is born of **the Spirit.**
KJV

I believe the scholars' understanding of what Christ said about the Spirit being like a breeze blowing influenced their interpretation of what was said in Genesis about Adam walking with God in the spirit of the day. They took it to mean the time of day when the cool breeze blows. Therefore, they translated the word cool of the day instead of spirit of the day.

The Spirit of the day is He that brings day to night or light to darkness. Now I want you to examine these scriptures that describe Christ.

Ask yourself, "Who is Peter talking about?"

2 Peter 1:19
19 We have also a more sure word of prophecy; whereunto ye do well that ye take heed, as unto a **light that shineth in a dark place,** until **the day dawn, and the day star arise in your hearts:**
KJV

The daystar is the Spirit of the day. When Zacharias was filled with the Holy Ghost and saw John the Baptist as a child, he prophesied of John and Christ. In the prophecy, he spoke of Christ being the Day Spring that brings light to darkness.

Luke 1:78-79
78 Through the tender mercy of our God; whereby **the dayspring from on high hath visited us,**
79 **To give light to them that sit in darkness and in the shadow of death**, to guide our feet into the way of peace.
KJV

Isa 60:1-3
60:1 Arise, shine; for thy light is come, and the glory of the LORD is risen upon thee.
2 For, behold, the darkness shall cover the earth, and gross darkness the people: but the LORD shall arise upon thee, and his glory shall be seen upon thee.
3 And the Gentiles shall come to thy light, and kings to the brightness of thy rising.
KJV

Again, understanding how metaphors work gives us the right understanding of who the Spirit of the day is, it is Christ. Therefore, when Adam was walking with God, he was walking with the Son, not the Father. This is confirmed in scripture.

No man has ever seen the father. None! I want you to get this very clear in your mind. Adam never saw the Father. The elders that ate before God never saw the Father. Moses, that saw God from the back, has never seen the Father. Let's go back to precept on precept, precept on precept, line line, and line line to get a full understanding of the truth of no man seeing the Father but Christ. Christ confirms this:

John 6:45-46
45 It is written in the prophets, And they **shall be all taught of God**. Every man therefore that hath heard, and hath learned of the Father, **cometh unto me**.
46 **Not that any man hath seen the Father, save he which is of God, he hath seen the Father.**
KJV

John understood that no man had ever seen the Father, and he knew whom they that claimed to have seen God had really seen.

John 1:18
18 No man hath seen God **at any time; the only begotten Son**, which is in the bosom of the Father, **he hath declared him**.
KJV

At any time are some strong words. The Father whose throne room exists in a place beyond the heavens has never been seen by any living man past or present, other than Christ.

I was sharing this revelation with a friend, Minister C.J. Akers Jr, when he told me he already knew it was Christ. When I asked him how he knew, he explained how God showed him that the voice of the Lord is Christ:

Gen 3:8
8 And they heard **the voice of the LORD God walking in the garden** in the cool of the day: and Adam and his wife hid themselves from the presence of the LORD God amongst the trees of the garden.
KJV

Christ is the part of the Father sent into the world to reveal all of the Father to men. It did not start when He came as the Lamb of God, it started long before that in the Garden of Eden.

The voice of God was walking in the Garden as the Spirit of the day, which is Christ. Adam and Eve were hiding and despite the question, God knew they were hiding. He also knew what took place. Over the years of experiencing God, I have learned that God will often ask us questions even though He already knows the answers. In most of my books, I share many experiences with the reader because I know the power of a testimony. Often it connects with someone going through a similar experience and will give them encouragement or an understanding that will set them free. Due to the format of this book, I have not shared as many of my experiences as usual. Yet, I do have a powerful testimony that I would like to share when God asked me a question that He already knew the answer to but like with Adam, His goal was to bring out the truth so I could understand the situation.

Samuel, do you love me?

I will never forget the day when Christ asked me that. People often believe that God talks to me everyday because of the testimonies that I frequently share, but that is not the case. He has spoken to me often but to put it in perspective, if you took everything He has said to me over my lifetime, you probably could not fill a 15-minute conversation. **The things that He says are short, simple, and powerful.** Often times, He will ask you a question that He knows you do not know the answer to but He wants you to think on it before He gives you the revelation. I have actually adopted this as my teaching style. Other times, the question is to reveal the state of your heart. Sometimes the question shakes you to the core as it did me that day.

Early in my Christian walk, I was a backslider. When Christ brought me back, He asked me if I loved Him. Some of you will not understand this but I started to cry and said, "That's not fair." See, I knew what is required to show we love Him, and I knew I was not there yet. I did not want to lie and say I loved Him, knowing the requirements of truly loving Christ. I did not want to tell the truth that I didn't because I still loved self more than Him. When I look back over the years, I see how He has kept me and has always done what was best for me, even when it was not what I wanted. Neither Christ nor the Father has ever broken a promise to me. It took a while for me to see that, like a child growing up upset with their father because of his strictness, only to find out they have survived and become a good person because of how their father raised them. That is when you appreciate your father. That is when you really, really love Him. You can let go of self and trust God in everything. I love God (Father, Son, and Holy Spirit), because He first loved me.

Nakedness

Adam hid himself because he did not want to face God. I want to share something with you about Adam and Eve's nakedness. Few people realize the Hebrew word used in Gen 2:25 and Gen 3:7, 10, 11 are two different words. "Arome" is used in chapter 2, and "Eyrom" in chapter 3 in the discussions about Adam's sin. The first word is used as a noun and the second as an adjective. The nakedness that Adam was created with was a description of his body having on no natural clothing, but the nakedness that he and Eve had after eating from the tree was because they had lost their spiritual covering. God did not lie when He said, "The day you eat from the tree you shall surely die." Nakedness is spiritual death and yes, I can prove it.

Luke 9:59-60
59 And he said unto another, Follow me. But he said, Lord, suffer me first to go and bury my father.
60 Jesus said unto him, **Let the dead bury their dead**: but go thou and preach the kingdom of God. KJV

Jesus told the young man to let the dead bury the dead. He was not talking about zombies burying dead people; He was speaking about the spiritually dead. Christ was calling the young man unto spiritual life, which is salvation. He indicated that the rest of his family who were unbelievers were spiritually dead. **Spiritually dead is the same as walking in nakedness.**

Rev 3:17-18
17 Because thou sayest, I am rich, and increased with goods, and have need of nothing; and knowest not that thou art wretched, and miserable, and poor, and blind, **and naked**:
18 I counsel thee to buy of me gold tried in the fire, that thou mayest be rich; and **white raiment, that thou mayest be clothed**, and that **the shame of thy nakedness** do not appear; and anoint thine eyes with eyesalve, that thou mayest see.
KJV

When Christ is speaking to the Laodicean church, which many believe reflects the end time church; He is speaking to a church full of unsaved people who don't even realize they are lost and spiritually dead. Earlier I showed how Christ used the healing of the blind man as a way of showing how salvation is received. **Being blind is also a metaphor for the spiritually dead.**

Please do not lose the understanding that the Garden story was a dark saying written to conceal information from the wicked. We will be going deeper into this understanding later in the book. The Word of God is the sword that hides the way to the tree of life. It is written to point you in many directions away from the entrance to the Garden if you do not have the Holy Spirit sent by Christ guiding you (more on this later).

God gave Adam and Eve clothes to put on because they were going to be put out of the Garden. Where they were going they would need clothing to protect them from the elements. Clothes were not needed in the Garden, so the nakedness that made him ashamed was not the lack of physical clothing. The nakedness that caused Adam to hide was the realization that he was spiritually dead and lost his covering. He lost his garments of righteousness and he was ashamed.

Jesus confirms this in Revelations:

Rev 16:15
15 Behold, I come as a thief. Blessed is he that watcheth, and **keepeth his garments, lest he walk naked, and they see his shame.**
KJV

I thank God for His mercy in my Christian walk. There have been times when I have walked away from the truth and God showed me my status in dreams and visions.

When I'm not wearing shoes or am looking for my shoes, He is telling me that I have walked out of the Gospel. My number one purpose in the Body of Christ is to spread the Gospel of Peace. When I allow other things to become my priority, I have lost my spiritual covering that protects me when I walk as a teacher of the Gospel.

When God shows me my feet uncovered, I know to check the message I am speaking to make sure it is inline with the gospel and not with self, or the things of this world:

Isa 52:7
7 **How beautiful upon the mountains are the feet of him that bringeth good tidings, that publisheth peace;** that bringeth good tidings of good, that publisheth salvation; that saith unto Zion, Thy God reigneth!
KJV

When I am walking with a carnal mind set in the flesh, He will show me wearing a green shirt. The green represents grass, a metaphor for the flesh.

Isa 40:6-8
6 The voice said, Cry. And he said, What shall I cry? **All flesh is grass, and all the goodliness thereof is as the flower of the field:**
7 The grass withereth, the flower fadeth: because the spirit of the LORD bloweth upon it: **surely the people is grass.**
8 The grass withereth, the flower fadeth: but the word of our God shall stand for ever.
KJV

When I am shown this, I know I need to do a search, and I will ask God to show me my sin so I can make the corrections.

When God shows me walking in dingy white clothes He is showing me my garment is dirty. I am engaged in sin, which is walking in iniquity (multiple sins). God does not give us garments that are dirty, wrinkled, or stained; if they have become that way, then **we have allowed them to by our actions.** Everyone in Christ has a garment. We put on salvation and received a white garment. When we sin we stain our garments, and some stains are harder to get out than others.

Now here is where the most dangerous part comes in. When God shows me in my underwear, I am in trouble. Your underwear is your garment of truth and it is the last thing to go before someone backslides or rejects Christ.

Eph 6:14
14 Stand therefore, having **your loins girt about with truth,** and having on the breastplate of righteousness;
KJV

Your loins are the area of your body that is covered by underwear, but metaphorically, it means your mind. Sometimes we are walking in sin, but we know the truth and have not yet been overcome by deception. When we lose our underwear, we are in total deception. We have lost all covering. We are naked. We have taken off our garments of salvation.

I thank God for His mercy that He has kept me and never shown me walking naked since He brought me back from a backslidden state almost twenty years ago. Because of the revelations I have received I have had some mighty fights and battles, but God has kept me. I have asked God never to allow me to justify my sin. Once you justify the sin, you will keep wallowing in the sin while sitting in the pit. You will not even notice when the dirt and grime completely dissolves away your garment of salvation. Then you will be walking naked like Adam hiding, and trying to cover your shame. Thank God, for the blood of Christ that washes sin away. If we embrace the truth and turn away from the sin, He has promised to wash us and put us back on the pathway of salvation.

1 John 2:1-2
2:1 My little children, these things write I unto you, that ye sin not. And if any man sin, we have an advocate with the Father, Jesus Christ the righteous:
2 And he is the propitiation for our sins: and not for ours only, but also for the sins of the whole world.
KJV

Before God can bring us back into right relationship with Him, we have to confess our sin without justification. This is what Adam did not do. He never asked for forgiveness, and he found justification for his sinful act. He blamed his wife instead of taking responsibility for his own actions and repenting:

Gen 3:9-12
9 And the LORD God called unto Adam, and said unto him, Where art thou?
10 And he said, I heard thy voice in the garden, and I was afraid, because I was naked; and I hid myself.
11 And he said, Who told thee that thou wast naked? Hast thou eaten of the tree, whereof I commanded thee that thou shouldest not eat?
12 And **the man said, The woman whom thou gavest to be with me, she gave me of the tree, and I did eat.**
KJV

Eve followed through with the same behavior, blaming the serpent for her accepting his deception. Even though she was initially deceived, she still knew she was not to talk to the devil (eat from the tree). She not only disobeyed by eating but also became a vessel to bring the same corrupt knowledge to her husband.

I often tell believers whom I teach, that compromising Christians are far more dangerous to us than sinners are. With sinners, we know what to expect so we put up our guards, but with brethren that are wallowing in sin, we have our guards down not realizing they can be used effectively by Satan to entrap us. They want others to be comfortable in the sin so they can justify their behavior. Therefore, they will go looking for others to participate in the sin so they can feel better that they are not the only one.

I do not want you to lose the understanding that you have gained so far. Remember, it was not a literal tree and the fruit was not a literal fruit. God said, "Who told you?" This statement again confirms that eating fruit from the tree is a metaphor for ingesting spoken knowledge. I believe (and this is me) that as soon as they both ingested the corrupt knowledge from Satan that Satan himself was the first to point out that they had lost their covering and were walking spiritually naked. Satan has always been the accuser of the brethren. After he has entrapped you in sin, he will be the first one there laughing at the state you're in and ridiculing you. He will tell you how disgusting and foolish you are and how easily you are deceived.

I can prove it to you. How many times have you fallen in sin and then heard thoughts in your mind telling you, "How are you going to pray to God with the mess you're in?" He will convince you that God is not going to hear your prayer because you're filthy. You will then go days without praying while he uses the time to pile more sins on you to get you so weighed down that you can never pray. **This is why it is so important to understand the mercy of God and how He is willing to forgive you. Just humble yourself, pray, and ask for forgiveness from a broken and contrite heart.** Once those steps are completed, rebuke the accusations of the enemy, then go and walk in holiness.

We have access to the Father even in times of sin because of the blood of Jesus. Never let the enemy fool you into hiding from God. He knows all and sees all. He wants us to come to Him and confess our sins. This is a form of humility that when done earnestly will not be rejected. Remember our High Priest is ever making intercession for us because He has experienced the fights we go through. Trust in the Word of God.

Heb 4:14-16
14 Seeing then that we have a great high priest, that is passed into the heavens, Jesus the Son of God, let us hold fast our profession.
15 For **we have not an high priest which cannot be touched with the feeling of our infirmities; but was in all points tempted like as we are, yet without sin.**
16 Let us therefore **come boldly unto the throne of grace, that we may obtain mercy, and find grace to help in time of need.**
KJV

We have something that Adam and Eve did not have. We have the blood of Jesus sprinkled on the mercy seat. Use it!

Chapter 8

I AM HE

It is the first day of the Biblical week and I am sitting alone in my room at five in the morning. For more than two weeks, I have been hearing this old time Christian song ringing in my ears: "Everybody got to know, everybody got to know, everybody got to know, who Jesus is. He's the Lilly of the valley. He's the brightest of all stars. He's the fairest of ten thousand. Everybody got to know."

Two times in prayer God has spoken to me and stated, "Finish the book!" Both times came after a week of conflict where it seemed nothing was going right. There have been a lot of distractions of the natural and spiritual type trying to hinder the completion of this book. I am actually sitting in a disaster zone after hurricane Irma swept through Florida leaving a ravaged landscape in its wake. Although my home and I came through the hurricane well, outside looks like someone dropped an atomic bomb. As I am writing this there are all kinds of matters on my mind of things I need to do but the things of God must always take priority.

This early morning is the first time I realized that God was not just telling me to hurry and finish the book but also that He wanted me to shine the light on who Christ is. The song in my mind was guidance, which I should have realized earlier. God wants everyone reading this to know who Jesus is. Who does the Word of God say He is?

The Father in the process of hiding Himself has also hid the true identity of who the Son really is but it is hidden in plain sight:

Isa 49:2
2 And **he hath made my mouth like a sharp sword; in the shadow of his hand hath he hid me**, and made me a polished shaft; in his quiver hath he hid me;
KJV

Isa 45:15-17
15 **Verily thou art a God that hidest thyself, O God of Israel, the Saviour.**
16 They shall be ashamed, and **also confounded, all of them: they shall go to confusion together** that are makers of idols.
17 But Israel shall be saved in the LORD with an everlasting salvation: ye shall not be ashamed nor confounded world without end.
KJV

If you created a microscopic world to achieve a planned goal and you needed to interact with this world on the microscopic level, it would be impossible because it is too small. You could possibly place it under a microscope and observe it but there could not be direct interaction because you and the world are on two different levels.

However, what would happen if you could make or give birth to a mini-micro you? This "you" is an exact copy of yourself on the same micro level of the created world. The mini-micro you would contain every essence of you but just on a level to fully interact in the microscopic world. This you would be your equal because He contained all that is in you. Yet if you asked Him who was greater, He would say, "He that I came out of is greater than I because I came forth from Him." You would call Him your Son and He would call you His Father.

What if you were way smarter than we could imagine and instead of creating the world and then giving birth to the mini-micro you to interact with it, **you were able to see from the beginning the ending.** Meaning before you did anything you knew everything you needed. Your first act was to give birth, or have **come forth** out of you, this part of you to interact with the micro world, and to be the facilitator in its creation. His purpose is the running of it from before the beginning of it. The mini-micro you would be your firstborn, because He came out of you. You didn't create Him. He came forth from out of you as an exact image of you on the micro level. Yet as the beginning process of everything, you are going to create. Even though you didn't create Him, you could call Him the beginning of creation. If you can understand, what I just expounded on, then it is your first step in understanding who Jesus is. Also, keep this in mind the micro world is not the earth. The micro world is the universe. Does scripture support what I am saying?

Paul not only gives us a clear picture of this he also identifies who he is speaking of as the head of the body the church, which is no other than Christ. Paul also points out that the fullness of the Father dwells in Him:

Col 1:15-19

15 Who is the image of the invisible God, the firstborn of every creature:

16 For by him were all things created, that are in heaven, and that are in earth, visible and invisible, whether they be thrones, or dominions, or principalities, or powers: all things were created by him, and for him:

17 And he is before all things, and by him all things consist.

18 And **he is the head of the body**, the church: who is the beginning, the firstborn from the dead; that in all things he might have the preeminence.

19 For **it pleased the Father that in him should all fulness dwell;** KJV

Christ testified that even though the fullness of all that is the Father was in Him, the Father was still His head and the Father was greater than Him:

John 14:28

28 Ye have heard how I said unto you, I go away, and come again unto you. If ye loved me, ye would rejoice, because I said, I go unto the Father: for my **Father is greater than I.**

Christ Himself testifies that He was the beginning process of everything that the Father created, not that He was created Himself because all through scripture it is shown He came out of the Father:

Rev 3:14
14 And unto the angel of the church of the Laodiceans write; These things saith the Amen, the faithful and true witness, **the beginning of the creation of God;**
KJV

Now that we have a deeper understanding of who Christ is, what did He mean by the statement **I AM HE?**

If you are feeling a little tired, I want you to take a short break because we are about to go real deep and I need your full attention to read the verses carefully. As always, I will wait for you right here (smile). I know, I know you want to finish. Trust me and take a break.

Welcome back. Ok, let's get started. Read this section of Isaiah 43 carefully:

Isa 43:10-16
10 Ye are my witnesses, saith the LORD, and my servant whom I have chosen: that ye may know and believe me, and understand that **I am he**: before me there was no God formed, neither shall there be after me.
11 **I, even I, am the LORD;** and **beside me there is no saviour.**
12 I have declared, and have saved, and I have shewed, when there was no strange god among you: therefore ye are my witnesses, saith the LORD, that I am God.
13 Yea, before the day was **I am he;** and there is none that can deliver out of my hand: I will work, and who shall let it?
14 Thus saith the LORD, your redeemer, the Holy One of Israel; For your sake I have sent to Babylon, and have brought down all their nobles, and the Chaldeans, whose cry is in the ships.
15 I am the LORD, your Holy One, the creator of Israel, your King.
16 Thus saith the LORD, **which maketh a way in the sea, and a path in the mighty waters;**
KJV

I want you to notice above that God uses the statement I AM HE twice. Yet more importantly, **I want you to note and remember that He mentions that He is the one that parted the sea (Red Sea).** He also points out that He is the only savior. There is no other besides Him.

Later on in the chapter, God indicates it is He that blotted out (erased) our sins for His own sake:

Isa 43:25
25 **I, even I, am he** that **blotteth out thy transgressions** for mine own sake, and will not remember thy sins.
KJV

Now let's move to chapter 51 of Isaiah. Again we see the "I, Even I, AM HE." God lets the believer know that He is the one that comforteth:

Isa 51:12-16
12 **I, even I, am he** that **comforteth** you: who art thou, that thou shouldest be afraid of a man that shall die, and of the son of man which shall be made as grass;
13 And forgettest the LORD thy maker, that hath stretched forth the heavens, and laid the foundations of the earth; and hast feared continually every day because of the fury of the oppressor, as if he were ready to destroy? and where is the fury of the oppressor?
14 The captive exile hasteneth that he may be loosed, and that he should not die in the pit, nor that his bread should fail.
15 But **I am the LORD thy God, that divided the sea, whose waves roared: The LORD of hosts is his name.**
16 And **I have put my words in thy mouth, and I have covered thee in the shadow of mine hand, that I may plant the heavens, and lay the foundations of the earth**, and say unto Zion, Thou art my people.
KJV

Did you get that? God said there is someone who He put His words in before He planted the heavens and laid the foundations of the earth. WHO IS THAT?

Isa 52:6-7

6 Therefore my people shall know my name: therefore they shall know in that day **that I am he** that doth speak: **behold, it is I**.

7 How beautiful upon the mountains are the feet of him that bringeth good tidings, that publisheth peace; that bringeth good tidings of good, that publisheth **salvation**; that saith unto Zion, Thy God reigneth!

KJV

Now God is talking about a person who is going to bring good tidings and publish salvation. He also identifies this person as coming to publish peace, which we know as the Gospel of Peace. **God actually identifies the person by name but as with many things, He hides the information in plain sight.**

Isa 52:10

10 **The LORD hath made bare his holy arm** in the eyes of all the nations; and all the ends of the earth shall see **the salvation of our God.**

KJV

The Hebrew word for "Salvation of our God" is Yehoshua or Yahshua, which is Christ's Hebrew name. God uses the metaphor of His Holy Arm to identify the person. This symbolism will be reinforced as we go further along. He makes bare his Holy ARM and calls Him YEHOSHUA. The original manuscripts for the scriptures had no numbers for chapters and verses in the books, so what you read will run into Isaiah 53. However, before that let's look at how God keeps describing this publisher of salvation whom He calls His Holy ARM and Yahshua:

Isa 52:13-15

13 Behold, my servant shall deal prudently, he shall be exalted and extolled, and be very high.

14 As many were astonied at thee; **his visage was so marred more than any man, and his form more than the sons of men:**

15 So shall **he sprinkle many nations**; the kings shall shut their mouths at him: for that which had not been told them shall they see; and that which they had not heard shall they consider.

KJV

Now I am going to show you why this CAN'T BE ISRAEL. This is the same servant who He calls His Holy Arm, who He put His words in His mouth before the foundation of the earth, so the foundation of the earth could be laid. Not ISRAEL! God continues talking about HIS SERVANT, which we know cannot be Israel. The detractors will give you all these scriptures where He called Israel His servant. He called David, Jacob, Abraham, Daniel, Cyrus, etc. (too many to list). However, none of them were around before the earth was and none of them is called the ARM OF THE LORD.

THE ARM OF THE LORD

Isa 53:1
53:1 Who hath believed our report? and to WHOM IS THE ARM OF THE LORD REVEALED?

I didn't want to get too scholarly in this book, because I am trying to break down some very deep things to the average believer. Nevertheless, I have to dedicate a page or two for those Jewish scholars, drawn to this book, to point out some things.

Many rabbis and other Jewish sources have been on a campaign to point out inconsistencies in the translations of the Hebrew text in most Bible editions. I do agree that there are some but very few. I also note that the high majority of the things that these Jewish sources want to point out have to do with Christ as the Messiah. I have refuted many of these accusations in debates.

I have also utilized the Dead Sea Scrolls to show that the Masorectic text used for most Tanachs (Hebrew Bibles) are filled with errors, yet the majority of practicing Jews believe the text is perfect. The Masorectic text is from 1100ce, a thousand years after Christ left and the apostles finished their last writings, and it can be easily proven to show that its arrangement was specifically to remove all evidence of Jesus (Yahshua) of Nazareth being the Messiah. This was the reason why the Dead Sea Scrolls were hidden away and not released for public view and examination for so many years. Although many have argued the contrary, those who have done a comparison with the Masorectic text can easily see that the Dead Sea

Scrolls exposes the hidden agenda of the translators of the Masorectic text.

The Masorectic text changed the scriptures to remove evidence of the Messiah in Isaiah 53 by turning HE and HIM to THEY and THEM so they could promote the deception and say it's Israel that the prophet is speaking about and not the Messiah. Yet the Talmud and almost all ancient Rabbis say the scripture is about the Messiah AND NOT Israel. Nevertheless, I will give you more proof. Notice again that the suffering servant is called Yehoshua in Isaiah 52:10 along with God's Holy ARM. Remember that verse of scripture that I said to remember when God said He parted the sea.

If the Arm of the Lord is Israel, then did Israel part the sea to let itself go through? On the other hand, did God as His Holy Arm called Yehoshua (salvation of God) part the sea to let Israel go through? Rahab is an ancient name for Egypt and we know who the dragon is who is working through Pharaoh:

Isa 51:9-10
9 Awake, awake, put on strength, **O arm of the LORD**; awake, as in the ancient days, in the generations of old. **Art thou not it that hath cut Rahab, and wounded the dragon?**
10 **Art thou not it which hath dried the sea, the waters of the great deep; that hath made the depths of the sea a way for the ransomed to pass over?**
KJV

The ARM OF THE LORD dried the sea so Israel could go over, so we know it is not ISRAEL.

Now let's go over what the scriptures say. The ARM OF THE LORD:
1. He is the suffering servant.
2. He is described as if a man.
3. He is going to be marred.
4. God put His words in His mouth to create the universe.
5. God calls Him salvation of God (Yehoshua in Hebrew/Jesus).
6. He struck Egypt and lead Israel through the sea.

WHO IS HE? Let's look at what else God says His Arm is going to do:

Isa 40:10-11
10 Behold, the Lord GOD will come with strong hand, and **his arm shall rule for him:** behold, his reward is with him, and his work before him.
11 **He shall feed his flock like a shepherd: he shall gather the lambs with his arm, and carry them in his bosom, and shall gently lead those that are with young.**
KJV

God foretells of the man that is His fellow, His Shepherd that is going to be stricken that dwells between the cherubims:

Zech 13:6-7
6 And one shall say unto him, **What are these wounds in thine hands?** Then he shall answer, Those with which I was wounded in the house of my friends.
7 **Awake, O sword, against my shepherd, and against the man that is my fellow,** saith the LORD of hosts: smite the shepherd, and the sheep shall be scattered: and I will turn mine hand upon the little ones.
KJV

Ps 80:1
80:1 To the chief Musician upon Sho-shan'-nim-E'-duth, A Psalm of A'-saph.
Give ear, **O Shepherd of Israel,** thou that leadest Joseph like a flock; **thou that dwellest between the cherubims,** shine forth.
KJV

Do you really know who Christ is? The knowledge of who Christ really is was hidden from the Pharisees because they were walking in unbelief. They did not want to believe He was the Messiah. Therefore, to even reach the deeper understanding of who He is, as He pointed to when He said, "I AM HE," was locked away from them. The unbelieving Jews then and now could not and cannot understand why Christ said, "I AM HE."

John 8:24
24 I said therefore unto you, that ye shall die in your sins: for if ye believe not that **I am he**, ye shall die in your sins.
KJV

Remember what Isaiah wrote:

Isa 29:9-14
9 Stay yourselves, and wonder; cry ye out, and cry: they are drunken, but not with wine; they stagger, but not with strong drink.
10 For **the LORD hath poured out upon you the spirit of deep sleep**, and hath closed your eyes: the prophets and your rulers, the seers hath he covered.
11 And the vision of all is become unto you as the words of **a book that is sealed**, which men deliver to one that is learned, saying, Read this, I pray thee: and he saith, **I cannot; for it is sealed:**
12 And the book is delivered to him that is not learned, saying, Read this, I pray thee: and he saith, I am not learned.
13 Wherefore the Lord said, Forasmuch as this people draw near me with their mouth, and with their lips do honour me, but have removed their heart far from me, and **their fear toward me is taught by the precept of men:**
14 Therefore, behold, I will proceed to do a marvellous work among this people, even a marvellous work and a wonder: for **the wisdom of their wise men shall perish, and the understanding of their prudent men shall be hid.**

God blinded the understanding of the people so they could not understand what was being revealed to them by the prophets and the rest of the Word of God. Their understanding was spiritually confined.

People miss the fact that God says the reason He is doing this is because men are accepting men's word on who He is, instead of God's Word. This is the same situation happening today where by if you hear people describe God, you have to seriously wonder if they even read the Bible. The God I hear people describe sounds like a big Santa Claus in the sky.

I once read a Facebook meme that summed it up perfectly: **"God is not who you say He is, He is who He says He is." Christ came to reveal to the world who God is. He is the image of God, the part of God sent to reveal all of God to men. You want to know God? Know Christ!** Christ's Words always go deeper than what they seem. When He speaks simple things and you study them, you realize they are way beyond simple. When He made the statement to the Jews that, "I AM HE," it goes way beyond Him just being the Messiah. Christ is the one and only part of God sent to reveal all of God to men. He is Lord of Lords and King of Kings. He is the image of the Father. When we see Him, we see the Father. He is God's mini me. He is God!

Chapter 9 *4-29-19*

Understanding The Curses

Gen 3:14-19

14 And the LORD God said unto the serpent, Because thou hast done this, thou art cursed above all cattle, and above every beast of the field; **upon thy belly shalt thou go, and dust shalt thou eat all the days of thy life:**

15 And I will put enmity between thee and the woman, and between thy seed and her seed; **it shall bruise thy head, and thou shalt bruise his heel.**

16 Unto the woman he said, **I will greatly multiply thy sorrow and thy conception; in sorrow thou shalt bring forth children; and thy desire shall be to thy husband, and he shall rule over thee.**

17 And unto Adam he said, Because thou hast hearkened unto the voice of thy wife, and hast eaten of the tree, of which I commanded thee, saying, Thou shalt not eat of it: **cursed is the ground for thy sake; in sorrow shalt thou eat of it all the days of thy life;**

18 **Thorns also and thistles shall it bring forth to thee; and thou shalt eat the herb of the field;**

19 **In the sweat of thy face shalt thou eat bread, till thou return unto the ground; for out of it wast thou taken: for dust thou art, and unto dust shalt thou return.**

KJV

I want to deal with a touchy subject about curses. There have been many writers producing books about how to come from under generational curses, the tithe curse, and curses from the enemy. I want you to read this carefully:

Prov 3:33
33 The curse of the LORD is in the house of the wicked: but he blesseth the habitation of the just.
KJV

There is no curse from God for those in Christ (walking in God's will). When God made the covenant with Israel and reaffirmed it before they entered the Promise Land, He had Moses place elders on two mountaintops to speak blessings and curses over the people. They had curses written into the Old Covenant, but what about the New Covenant?

Most Christians are not aware of the fact that Jesus gave the New Covenant in the Sermon on the Mount. He literally gave the terms for those who are in the Body of Christ. **Matthew chapters 5, 6, 7 contain the Law of Liberty, which is the Law of the New Covenant written in your heart.** You will find no curses in this covenant. Christ has delivered us from the curses. He emphasized this in the way He started His doctrine of the covenant:

Matt 5:1-12
5:1 And seeing the multitudes, he went up into a mountain: and when he was set, his disciples came unto him:
2 And he opened his mouth, and taught them, saying,
3 **Blessed** are the poor in spirit: for theirs is the kingdom of heaven.
4 Blessed are they that mourn: for they shall be comforted.
5 Blessed are the meek: for they shall inherit the earth.
6 Blessed are they which do hunger and thirst after righteousness: for they shall be filled.
7 Blessed are the merciful: for they shall obtain mercy.
8 Blessed are the pure in heart: for they shall see God.
9 Blessed are the peacemakers: for they shall be called the children of God.
10 Blessed are they which are persecuted for righteousness' sake: for theirs is the kingdom of heaven.
11 Blessed are ye, when men shall revile you, and persecute you, and shall say all manner of evil against you falsely, for my sake.
12 Rejoice, and be exceeding glad: for great is your reward in heaven: for so persecuted they the prophets which were before you. KJV

The first word that came out of Christ's mouth was, **"blessed."** Christ mentions the word "curse" three times in scripture, twice to tell believers that we should bless those that curse us and once in the parable about the sheep and the goat (Matt 25:41) to show God casting the goats into everlasting fire prepared for the devil and his angels.

The curses of the Law, the enemy, those given by God in the Garden for Adam (all mankind), and Eve (women) have no effect on those in Christ who are walking in His will.

The Law with its curses was added because of the transgressions of the people of Israel. Christ came to bring a New Covenant written in our hearts, which contains no curse for those under the New Covenant.

Gal 3:13-19

13 Christ hath redeemed us **from the curse of the law**, being made a curse for us: for it is written, Cursed is every one that hangeth on a tree:

14 That the blessing of Abraham might come on the Gentiles through Jesus Christ; that **we might receive the promise of the Spirit through faith.**

15 Brethren, I speak after the manner of men; Though it be but a man's covenant, **yet if it be confirmed, no man disannulleth, or addeth thereto.**

16 Now to Abraham and his seed were the promises made. He saith not, And to seeds, as of many; **but as of one, And to thy seed, which is Christ.**

17 And this I say, that the covenant, that was confirmed before of God in Christ, the law, which was four hundred and thirty years after, cannot disannul, that it should make the promise of none effect.

18 For if the inheritance be of the law, it is no more of promise: but God gave it to Abraham by promise.

19 **Wherefore then serveth the law? It was added because of transgressions, till the seed should come to whom the promise was made;** and it was ordained by angels in the hand of a mediator. KJV

To get a deeper understanding on this please see my book "Curses and Lies Truth and Tithes."

The enemy of your soul cannot curse those in Christ. He can trick you into believing you're cursed or he can deceive you into walking outside of Christ and coming back under the curses of Adam, and the Law. If you are walking in right relationship with God IN Christ, then no curse can affect you. If God has blessed you, then no one can curse you:

Num 22:12
12 And God said unto Balaam, Thou shalt not go with them; **thou shalt not curse the people: for they are blessed.**
KJV

Num 23:23
23 **Surely there is no enchantment against Jacob, neither is there any divination against Israel**: according to **this time** it shall be said of Jacob and of Israel, What hath God wrought!
KJV

There is a great revelation in the story of Balaam when he was hired by King Balak to curse Israel (Num 22). What is revealed is that no enchantment or divination (curse/witchcraft) can work against those walking in God's will. This is why the enemy works so hard to keep us in sin and iniquity. This is also, why it is so important that when we fall in sin we need to come boldly (and quickly) to the throne of grace to repent, ask forgiveness, and or seek mercy. Do not wallow in sin.

Yes, the enemy and his minions will send curses, witchcraft, sorcery, and demons our way and we will receive attacks. Know the Word of God, address the attack with the Word, and rebuke it. It must go. **When we don't know the authority we have by walking in God's will, then the enemy will act as if he doesn't know either. Do not let him fool you, he knows; he is just overjoyed when we do not know.**

Now we must also be aware not to invite curses on ourselves by embracing the things of Satan, or by going into his area of operation when we were not sent by God. You can't take Satan's basketball and then tell him he can't play in the game. If it is his ball then he can play. Too many Christians have items in their home that belong to the enemy and then wonder why he's in their home. You invited him in.

Our authority starts now, not when we enter the Kingdom of God when it finally manifests on the earth. We enter into the Kingdom when the Spirit of God baptizes us into the Body. If you are in Christ, you are already in the Kingdom and that means none of the curses from God can be applied to you.

Rev 22:3-4

3 And **there shall be no more curses**: but the throne of God and of the Lamb shall be in it; and his servants shall serve him:
4 And they shall see his face; and his name shall be in their foreheads.
KJV

Therefore, if any man, to include those in ministry, tells you that you are cursed, correct them with the Word and then bless them.

Eve's Curse

Gen 3:16
16 Unto the woman he said, **I will greatly multiply thy sorrow and thy conception; in sorrow thou shalt bring forth children; and thy desire shall be to thy husband, and he shall rule over thee**.
KJV

I want to start our discussions on the curses in the Garden with Eve, so I can leave the curse on Satan (serpent) for last. This is necessary because understanding Adam's curse is going to allow us to better understand Satan's curse.

The curse that fell on Eve was that she would not only have sorrow (pain) in childbirth but through the whole pregnancy. Non-believers that often like to ridicule the Bible need to compare the pregnancy of animals and their birth with what women go through. This alone should confirm the truth of the Bible. I have seen many animal births. They compare in no way to the struggle of human birth. You will see animals at full term running through the wild yet many women at full term have difficulty getting off the couch. There is no doubt that something took place with women that separated them from the normalcy of birth in other animals.

Every woman of God is released from the curse of Eve. The problem is, you are still suffering from the curse. The issue is, you do not know you are free and/or you are not walking in love and the will of God. The solution is to correct the issues, confess the truth of no curse in Christ, and walk in freedom.

I want to share a revelation with you. **Women of God do not have to go through the pains of pregnancy and childbirth as other women.** If you are pregnant or plan to be pregnant, continually pray through the pregnancy affirming that the curse of Eve does not apply to you. Then you need to walk in faith, love, holiness, and sobriety through the pregnancy and watch what happens. You will be amazed. Even though the serpent deceived Eve, she was still in transgression. Yet Paul leaves a word confirming the removal of the curse in the verses below.

1 Tim 2:14-15
14 And Adam was not deceived, but the woman being deceived was in the transgression.
15 Notwithstanding **she shall be saved in childbearing, if they continue in faith and charity and holiness with sobriety.**
KJV

I remember reading about those who were saying women had to bear a child to be saved. Wow! I have even heard women repeat this misunderstanding of what Paul was saying. **What Paul is speaking about is that a woman can be saved from the pain of childbirth because Paul realizes that the curse is cancelled for those in Christ.** If you're still suffering through pregnancy or have suffered through the birth of a child while a Christian, then there is a simple problem that can be corrected.

The problem is twofold. Many women do not know this so the enemy uses pregnancy to afflict them with pain. For years, I suffered with pain in my feet, which people tried to get me to accept as gout, the foot ailment. They even told me that it was genetic because my father had the disease. I almost believed them until I realized I was overlooking the obvious. My father was my stepfather, not my biological father, so how could it be genetic? Thank God for increasing my spiritual discernment. I noticed I would feel a spirit moving on my foot just before the pain and swelling started.

As the Holy Spirit started teaching me, what was really going on, He took me back to when I heard a sermon from an anointed bishop who had a powerful deliverance ministry. He preached on how he noticed that when he would cast demons out of some people the sickness or disease they were dealing with would go away also. He realized it was a spirit of infirmity that was causing the sickness and the symptoms mirrored an everyday sickness. The people just accepted they had the disease, and took medication to control the symptoms. I started observing the pattern of when I would feel a spirit attach to my body and how long it would take the area to start giving me pain. Once I realized what was happening, I started utilizing the sword of the Spirit to speak the Word against the demon, it would leave, and all the pain and swelling would go away.

I had been suffering for years with this and all the time it was a demon, not gout. The enemy is crafty. If you don't realize that as a believer walking in God's will that you have been delivered from the sorrow of pregnancy and childbirth, then they will come right in and mimic the symptoms to cause you affliction. Line up with God's word in all facets of your life, then speak the promise of the removal of all curses and watch what a pleasant experience your pregnancy will be. Believe God's Word above all and rebuke the demon of pain and sorrow.

The second issue why so many women of God are still suffering through pregnancy and childbirth is due to not lining up with what Apostle Paul said about faith, charity (love), holiness, and sobriety. If you are not walking in these things, then you cannot claim the promise. If you know what is needed just practice until you are able to walk in the fullness of these things. The more we operate in something the better we get at it, and the more we are able to do it. This is one of the main reasons some grow and reach spiritual maturity while others are stagnant in their spiritual walk. Practice makes perfect.

God said, "Thy desire shall be to thy husband, and he shall rule over thee." This can be a touchy subject for Christians. Men point to this scripture to confirm they have rule over their wives and women in general. Women point to this to say it was a curse that is lifted, so they no longer have to obey their husbands. To understand the curse, you have to realize that the word translated "rule" means to be like a king over your subjects. It has a sense of domineering or lording over someone. This is the same rule that God stated to Cain that sin would have over him if he desired it. (For a better understanding of what took place with Cain, Adam's son, please see "Assault on Innocence," and read the chapter on guarding your mouth.) The curse was going to make women long after (desire) men, and men would domineer over them. This is not the relationship that God intended for men and women. Eve was the other half of Adam. She came out of him and was part of him. When people read about the relationship between men and women in the Bible, they forget that they were still under the curse.

A perfect example of how the relationship was supposed to be before sin is shown in the relationship of Christ and His Body, the Church. Know this, that it is required that all men who call on the name of the Lord, treat their wives in the same manner that is laid out by Paul concerning Christ and His Body. If you're not doing this, then you're out of order. You are hindering your spiritual growth and your wife's.

Eph 5:25-32
25 Husbands, love your wives, even as Christ also loved the church, and gave himself for it;
26 That he might sanctify and cleanse it with the washing of water by the word,
27 That he might present it to himself a glorious church, not having spot, or wrinkle, or any such thing; but that it should be holy and without blemish.
28 So ought men to love their wives as their own bodies. He that loveth his wife loveth himself.

29 For no man ever yet hated his own flesh; but nourisheth and cherisheth it, even as the Lord the church:

30 For **we are members of his body, of his flesh, and of his bones.**

31 For this cause shall a man leave his father and mother, and shall be joined unto his wife, and they two shall be one flesh.

32 **This is a great mystery: but I speak concerning Christ and the church.**

KJV

Women, you have to understand something, this part of Eve's curse fell on women and men. **Just as Adam's curse fell on all humankind, Eve's curse did also.** The role the man plays is to have a nature that wants to domineer over women. If you are saved and sanctified but your husband is not, realize that just because you are freed from the curse does not mean he is. This is why we do not marry the unsaved. Every time we are yoked together with unbelievers, we have to realize that they are still cursed. They will react and act according to the curses over their lives. That is why they act the way they do.

In saying all of that the question remains, "Does a man still have headship over his wife?" Yes, he does. The man is still the final authority over the family with Christ being his headship and authority. Paul confirms this in the last verse of Eph 5:

Eph 5:33

33 Nevertheless **let every one of you in particular so love his wife even as himself;** and **the wife see that she reverence her husband.**

KJV

We work together as a team just like the Body of Christ but each person has to understand the role they play and give their all in that assigned role. Remember it is temporary for a husband and wife because there are no husbands and wives in heaven, just sons of God.

Please notice that Eve's curse affected her function and her purpose as mother. Why I point this out will become more evident as we deal with Adam's and the serpent's curse.

Adam's curse

Gen 3:17-19

17 And unto Adam he said, Because thou **hast hearkened unto the voice of thy wife,** and hast eaten of the tree, of which I commanded thee, saying, Thou shalt not eat of it: **cursed is the ground for thy sake; in sorrow shalt thou eat of it all the days of thy life;**

18 **Thorns also and thistles shall it bring forth to thee; and thou shalt eat the herb of the field;**

19 **In the sweat of thy face shalt thou eat bread,** till thou return unto the ground; for out of it wast thou taken: for **dust thou art, and unto dust shalt thou return.**

KJV

We have to be spiritual minded when reading the curse of Adam to get the full understanding. There is a literal meaning, and a spiritual aspect, to the curse. God points out that Adam listened to his wife. He was not deceived. He sinned willingly. **It is not a problem to listen to one's wife; it is a problem when we allow a wife or anyone else to persuade us into disobeying God.** When the devil cannot get to you directly, he will do it indirectly by speaking through others.

Job's wife

I want to share a revelation with you showing how the enemy can use others as weapons against us. In the book of Job (originally called The Repentant One), we read a dialogue that takes place between Job and his wife. Pay attention to what she says:

Job 2:9-10

9 Then said his wife unto him, **Dost thou still retain thine integrity? Curse God, and die.**

10 But he said unto her, Thou speakest as one of the foolish women speaketh. What? Shall we receive good at the hand of God, and shall we not receive evil? In all this did not Job sin with his lips.
KJV

Now Job's wife wants him to curse God so he will die. She says this because of all the suffering he is going through, and it would seem that she thinks it's better for him to just die rather continue suffering. **As Christians we have to always have our spiritual ears open and allow discernment to filter everything we see, hear, and speak.** Sometimes things are not what they seem. The enemy of our souls is crafty, and many times when we think we are having a discussion with a loved one that is speaking foolishly against the things of God, we are actually speaking to a demon or the devil himself. Now pay attention to this discourse between God and Satan:

Job 2:3
3 And the LORD said unto Satan, Hast thou considered my servant Job, that there is none like him in the earth, a perfect and an upright man, one that feareth God, and escheweth evil? And **still he holdeth fast his integrity**, although thou movedst me against him, to destroy him without cause.
KJV

Did you see it? If you did not notice anything, read it one more time, I will wait right here for you.

You're back? That was quick! Ok. God mentions to Satan that Job is holding fast his integrity. Where is Job's wife during this conversation? Nowhere! This conversation is being held in the presence of God. **How is it that she asks Job the very same thing that God proclaimed? Do you still hold your integrity?** This is not a coincidence that she questions the exact thing that God proclaimed about Job. It was not his wife speaking; it was Satan speaking through her to discourage Job so he would curse God. This old trick is still being used today when Satan uses those closest to us to cause separation between us and God, so we can be overcome. I believe it was the same thing with Eve. We have to be cautious of the fruit of the lips coming from others to persuade us. Sometimes it is not the person talking; it is the tree of the knowledge of good and evil speaking through them. We have to learn how to differentiate between the two trees. Who is speaking? Is it death or life? Can you tell?

Prov 15:4
4 **A wholesome tongue is a tree of life**: but **perverseness therein is a breach in the spirit.**
KJV

    The proverb is talking about the effects of speaking death and life. The word "breach" is taken from the Hebrew word "*Sheber*", which is also translated as destruction. The word translated perverseness "*celeph*" comes from a root meaning to distort or subvert. This is what came from Satan's mouth, which caused the death of Adam's spirit. Satan gets to Adam indirectly through his wife and he embraces the fruit of death.

    Adam blamed his wife for his sin but God knew that Adam's problem was not Eve it was Adam himself. Look at this:

Prov 18:21-22
21 Death and life are in the power of the tongue: and they that love it shall eat the fruit thereof.
22 **Whoso findeth a wife findeth a good thing**, and obtaineth favour of the LORD.
KJV

    A wife is a good thing but a man has to nurture his wife as her head. You can't blame others for your sin. **We all have to stand before God to answer for what we have done in the body.** Adam should have taken responsibility for his actions and repented. He should have stood in the gap for his wife, and not accuse her. The proverb points out that you will eat the fruit from whatever you love, either death or life. Adam ate the fruit because he wanted to.

The Ground

    The curse of God falls on Adam and directly attaches to his purpose.

Gen 2:15
15 And the LORD God took the man, and put him into the garden of Eden to dress it and to keep it.
KJV

Adam was a farmer by vocation assigned to take care of the Garden. Moreover, just as the curse that fell on Eve was according to her purpose as a child bearer, Adam's curse affects his purpose as a gardener. God cursed the ground. Now we know this is the physical ground because years after, the curse still stands. On the birth of Noah, it's noted that Noah would bring comfort because of the accursed ground:

Gen 5:29
29 And he called his name Noah, saying, This same shall comfort us concerning our work and toil of our hands, **because of the ground which the LORD hath cursed.**
KJV

We learned earlier how the curse was removed after the flood, which actually may point to this verse being a prophecy of Noah causing the curse to be removed (indirectly).

There was a literal meaning of the curse, but I want to show you that there was also a spiritual meaning. Part of the curse is that the ground would bring forth thorns and thistles (briers) unto Adam, but this was not just the literal ground. Adam himself would produce the thorns and thistles also. Again, remember Adam was taken from the ground.

Gen 3:18
18 **Thorns also and thistles** shall it bring forth to thee; and thou shalt eat the herb of the field;
KJV

The curse gave thorns and thistles access to the ground of his flesh. Demons could enter his body:

2 Cor 12:7

7 And lest I should be exalted above measure through the abundance of the revelations, there was given to me **a thorn in the flesh, the messenger of Satan** to buffet me, lest I should be exalted above measure.

KJV

If I said a messenger of God, everyone would know it was an angel. So what do you think is a messenger from Satan?

2 Tim 2:25-26

25 In meekness instructing those that oppose themselves; if God peradventure will give them repentance to the acknowledging of the truth;

26 And that they may recover themselves out of **the snare** of the devil , **who are taken captive by him at his will.**

KJV

Satan's kingdom operates in two areas of the body, thorns in the flesh and snares in the soul. Thorns in the flesh are demons that we give access to when we sin whether in thoughts, words, or deeds. When we give into the desires of the flesh, they enter in. For those who are questioning thoughts as sins, remember that Christ said lusting after a woman is adultery in the heart. You also have snares for the soul, which deals with a deception that we have embraced. These demons enter in through the deception and operate like doorkeepers to keep the doorways to fleshly sins open. They keep us sowing to the flesh and reaping thorns and nestles:

Gal 6:7-8

7 Be not deceived; God is not mocked: for whatsoever a man soweth, that shall he also reap.

8 For **he that soweth to his flesh shall of the flesh reap corruption;** but he that soweth to the Spirit shall of the Spirit reap life everlasting.

KJV

Remember, you're sowing seeds of knowledge and whatever you sow in your garden is what you're going to harvest.

Heb 6:6-8

6 If they shall fall away, to renew them again unto repentance; seeing they crucify to themselves the Son of God afresh, and put him to an open shame.

7 For the earth which drinketh in the rain that cometh oft upon it, and bringeth forth herbs meet for them by whom it is dressed, receiveth blessing from God:

8 But **that which beareth thorns and briers is rejected, and is nigh unto cursing; whose end is to be burned.**
KJV

Instead of having the tree of life growing in him, Adam chooses thorns and thistles. As Christians, if we keep sowing wickedness in our hearts it is going to bring forth wickedness in our speech and actions. As the seeds of thorns and thistles grow, they will be transforming our souls into their image.

Adam was also told that he would eat the herb of the field, and this too has a spiritual meaning. The Bible talks about God creating fruit trees, herbs, and grass. We have already established that fruit tree is metaphor for the spirit and grass is a metaphor for the flesh. What are herbs a metaphor for? You got it, it's the soul.

An unredeemed soul is full of the carnal knowledge of this world. God cursed Adam and limited him to only being able to digest carnal knowledge. He eats herbs from the field, meaning he would only be able to ingest carnal knowledge, which is what the soul produces. Instead of eating from the spirit (tree) and being able to ingest spiritual things, God cursed him to only be able to ingest the carnal knowledge of the soul (herbs).

Sidenote: When the Bible speaks of the heart (not the natural heart), it is referring to the mind and soul they are all interchangeable.

Before the fall, Adam had a living spirit and was able to understand spiritual things. Remember, there was a natural manifestation with the ground being cursed but the ground was healed. However, the state of the carnal heart (mind) of man was revealed to still be in an accursed condition:

Gen 8:21-22

21 And the LORD smelled a sweet savour; and the LORD said in his heart, **I will not again curse the ground any more** for man's sake; **for the imagination of man's heart is evil from his youth;** neither will I again smite any more every thing living, as I have done.
22 While the earth remaineth, seedtime and harvest, and cold and heat, and summer and winter, and day and night shall not cease.
KJV

It was hard to produce right knowledge because the ground of his heart was cursed. Everything the carnal unredeemed man sees is according to his carnal nature because his spirit is dead. Even after salvation, there is a growth period where we are still holding on to this carnal mindset. Christ exposed this issue.

Mark 8:15-21

15 And he charged them, saying, **Take heed, beware of the leaven of the Pharisees, and of the leaven of Herod.**
16 And they reasoned among themselves, saying, It is because we have no bread.
17 And when Jesus knew it, he saith unto them, Why reason ye, because ye have no bread? perceive ye not yet, neither understand? have ye your heart yet hardened?
18 **Having eyes, see ye not? and having ears, hear ye not? and do ye not remember?**
19 When I brake the five loaves among five thousand, how many baskets full of fragments took ye up? They say unto him, Twelve.
20 And when the seven among four thousand, how many baskets full of fragments took ye up? And they said, Seven.
21 And he said unto them, **How is it that ye do not understand?**
KJV

Christ used the metaphor leaven (used to make bread) when speaking of knowledge, yet the disciples thought He was speaking about the natural bread. Carnal minds cannot understand spiritual things and babes in Christ are slow to understand. The knowledge of the Pharisees and Herod was corrupt. Carnal minds understand that the natural bread sustains our bodies and we need it to live in this life. Spiritual minded people understand that the Word of God is spiritual bread and we need it to attain and maintain our spiritual life.

Luke 4:4

4 And Jesus answered him, saying, It is written, **That man shall not live by bread alone, but by every word of God.**
KJV

This is why it is imperative that we have a mindset to push the Gospel of Peace to unbelievers before we try to teach them the deeper things of God. The deeper things of God will only be twisted and corrupted by them because their hearts are still cursed. They cannot discern (understand) the things of God beyond salvation. Until their spirits are born again, they will only produce thorns and thistles.

1 Cor 2:14

14 But **the natural man receiveth not the things of the Spirit of God: for they are foolishness unto him: neither can he know them, because they are spiritually discerned.**
KJV

Earlier in Hebrews 6:6-8 we learned that the production of thorns and briers (thistles) is a metaphor for what is brought forth by the unsaved. The writer of Hebrews even indicates that it is a curse. Adam passed on this curse to all his descendants and the curse is on the heads of all those not in relationship with God. **ALL!** Here are the questions we must ask, "What is the fruit produced by thorns and thistles?" What seed of knowledge do they produce?

Matt 13:22

22 He also that received seed **among the thorns** is he that heareth the word; and the care of this world, and the deceitfulness of riches, choke the word, and he becometh unfruitful.
KJV

In the parable of the sower, Christ shows us that the seed He planted is the Word of God that grows and produces fruits of righteousness. Yet, He also points us toward the identity of the thorns by saying it has to do with the cares of this world and the deceit of riches. Remember that the fruit produced by the thorns is knowledge of the cares of this world, and the deceitfulness of riches

Good vs. Corrupt tree

Back in chapter three, I touched on these verses:
Luke 6:43-45
43 For a **good tree bringeth not forth corrupt fruit; neither doth a corrupt tree bring forth good fruit.**
44 For **every tree is known by his own fruit. For of thorns men do not gather figs, nor of a bramble bush gather they grapes.**
45 A good man out of the good treasure of his heart bringeth forth that which is good; and **an evil man out of the evil treasure of his heart bringeth forth that which is evil: for of the abundance of the heart his mouth speaketh.**
KJV

  I have been told over the years that I look deep into things, but I realize this is the mindset given to me by God to understand His Word as a teacher in the Body of Christ. When I see peculiar things or things that do not seem to make sense, I start digging. I believe I am a good man and a man of God, but over the years, there have been times when I let foolishness come out of my mouth. I have also seen people who walk in wickedness speak a word of wisdom. Every good man (tree) has spoken corrupt knowledge at one time or another. Therefore, when Christ said a good tree cannot produce corrupt fruit, it did not make sense to me. I knew He was talking about what they speak because the last verse above states, "For of the abundance of the heart his mouth speaketh." I know the Word of God does not lie; every word spoken out of the mouth of the Father (and Christ) is the truth. I knew there had to be something I was missing. The Holy Spirit rewarded my search through scripture by guiding me to the truth:

1 Peter 3:4
4 But let it be **the hidden man of the heart, in that which is not corruptible, even the ornament of a meek and quiet spirit,** which is in the sight of God of great price.
KJV

The seed is the Word of God planted in our hearts. The Word of God is Spirit; it becomes one with our spirit man, and they are not corruptible. That is why Christ came to save our souls and not our spirits. Our spirits do not need saving, they do not sin.

1 Peter 1:23

23 **Being born again, not of corruptible seed, but of incorruptible, by the word of God, which liveth and abideth for ever.**
KJV

Spiritual Growth

Remember when I said earlier in the book that as you open a door with a key of knowledge you would enter a room of understanding, which will have other keys that open other doors? I realized that the tree planted by God comes from an incorruptible seed, which is the Word of God, and our born again spirit. The tree is the spirit operating in you. Now I got the key to understanding another scripture that had always puzzled me.

1 John 3:9

9 Whosoever is born of God doth not commit sin; for his seed remaineth in him: **and he cannot sin**, because he is born of God.
KJV

I remember watching a woman testify that even when she sinned; it was not sin because the Bible said those that are born again do not sin. She was using the scripture to justify that her sins did not matter, and don't count, because she is born again. She was justifying a sinful lifestyle by the misappropriation (wrong application) of scripture.

I did not understand the scripture at the time because I knew I was a born again believer, and I sinned. I was growing and sinning less and less, as I grew spiritually, but to say that my sins did not count, I knew was a lie from the pit of hell. I did not understand the scripture until I got the key.

Our souls and flesh are not born again only the spirit man, which cannot sin. Our spirits will never sin, and if our spirit is leading us to sin it is not a born again Christ like seed, it is a demon. Ladies and gentlemen, your spirit cannot sin, and when your soul transforms, conforms, and purifies itself into the image of Christ, it will stop sinning also. The problem with the soul is that it will conform to whatever spirit you are obeying, and if it is a demonic spirit, then your soul will become more and more corrupt. The soul is corruptible.

Have you ever watched a plant grow? When you put a seed in the dirt, it can literally sense that it is in soil and will start to grow. Most of the time the germination (growth process) starts as water saturates the soil. Farmers will tell you that you can speed up some seeds' germination by first soaking them in water. In the spiritual, we soak God's seed in living waters. The seed will consume the dirt around it, transforming the dirt into the form of the tree. As the tree grows, it consumes more and more dirt. The transformation process is generated and maintained by the presence of water. No water, no growth. The living water that we ingest causes the spirit man to grow, transforming the soul into the image of Christ while consuming (killing) the flesh (dirt). When we have a full understanding of the process and the importance of staying in Christ so that the living waters keep pouring, then we will have the full understanding of spiritual growth. There is **no** spiritual growth outside of Christ, which is our union with God the Father. When Adam sinned, he was cut off from God and died spiritually. That is why all humanity needs to be born again. **It is a spiritual birth that restarts this process of spiritual growth until we are transformed into the image of Christ.**

I like to share testimonies in my books and for those who have read some of my other books you can testify to this. Due to the format and subject matter that I am writing about in this book, it contains fewer testimonies than usual. Therefore, I love when I get an opportunity to add one that compliments the subject that is being discussed.

As a young Christian, I often meditated on scriptures about the makeup of our bodies. The clearest picture of understanding I received on our makeup came from a mango. I have been eating mangoes all my life and can describe the seed to you perfectly. The seed is oval and white in appearance with ridges running the length of it. It has fibrous hair on it, and is hard and flat. At least that is what I thought. One day as I was eating a mango, I got in my spirit that I needed to open the seed. As I pried the seed open with a knife, I got the shock of my life. Inside of the thing I thought was the seed, was something that looked like a little green lima bean. It was the real seed that was hidden inside a husk (what I described), which most people think is the seed. God was showing me that the hidden spiritual man dwells in our soul and most people are identifying the soul as the spirit but they are wrong.

The part of the mango that we eat is the flesh, which contains a husk that represents the soul. Inside, hidden away, is the seed that represents the spirit man. There are so many wonders in nature to look upon that reveals how things work in the spirit realm. This is God's signature on His handiwork, left so we of this world will know there is a God.

Rom 1:19-20
19 Because that which may be known of God is manifest in them; for God hath shewed it unto them.
20 For the invisible things of him from the creation of the world are clearly seen, **being understood by the things that are made**, even his eternal power and Godhead; so that they are without excuse: KJV

Our body is created from the dust (soil) of the ground, and a spirit that is planted in this dirt grows until it produces fruit containing seed of itself. If you eat fruit from the tree of life, the spirit in you will contain the DNA of a tree of life, and will grow into a tree of life itself producing fruit. When Christ said a corrupt tree could not produce good fruit, He was saying that a demonic spirit speaking through a person will always speak corrupt knowledge. Whatever is in the depth of your heart will speak through your mouth. **That is why we are commanded to test the spirit speaking through ourselves, prophets, pastors, or anyone else by asking it to confess that Christ has come in the flesh. We do not ask the person to confess, we ask the spirit speaking** through them. **Let me also add that if a voice in your head is speaking to you, then when you ask it to confess that Christ came in the flesh, if it goes silent, then a demon was just speaking to you.** Testing the spirit, or rather the lack of testing, is one reason there is so much deception in the Christian church today. Everybody is hearing from God, but very few are testing the spirit (or even know how to do it).

2 John 7
7 For many deceivers are **entered** into the world, **who confess not that Jesus Christ is come in the flesh.** This is a deceiver and an antichrist.
KJV

1 John 4:2-3
2 Hereby know ye the Spirit of God: **Every spirit** that confesseth that Jesus Christ is come in the flesh is of God:
3 And **every spirit** that confesseth not that Jesus Christ is come in the flesh is not of God: and this is that spirit of antichrist, whereof ye have heard that it should come; and **even now already is it in the world.**
KJV

People are waiting on the antichrist not realizing that it is a spirit, there are many of them, and they have been here for a long time.

Example of testing: "Spirit that is speaking to me do you confess that Jesus Christ, Yehoshua, the Son, and Word of God who is God's salvation, has come in the flesh?" If you hear a confession (not just yes but a confession), then the spirit speaking to you is of God. If you get silence, growling, or an explanation that leaves out confession, then rebuke it. If the churches practiced this, many of these so-called prophets would sit down.

Back to the thorns and thistles:

Matt 7:16-23
16 Ye shall know them by their fruits. **Do men gather grapes of thorns, or figs of thistles?**

17 Even so every good tree bringeth forth good fruit; but a corrupt tree bringeth forth evil fruit.

18 A good tree cannot bring forth evil fruit, neither can a corrupt tree bring forth good fruit.

19 Every tree that bringeth not forth good fruit is hewn down, and cast into the fire.

20 Wherefore by their fruits ye shall know them.

21 Not every one that saith unto me, Lord, Lord, shall enter into the kingdom of heaven; but he that doeth the will of my Father which is in heaven.

22 Many will say to me in that day, Lord, Lord, have we not prophesied in thy name? and in thy name have cast out devils? and in thy name done many wonderful works?

23 And then will I profess unto them, I never knew you: depart from me, ye that work iniquity.

KJV

When the above verses are read, it is easy to get the understanding that the fruit from the thorns and thistles represent what a person does. Christ goes from saying, "By their fruits ye shall know them," into talking about those that work iniquity will be rejected. Remember, the fruit is more than what a carnal mind speaks; it is what is spoken through the person by the spirits taking up residence in them. It is the wisdom and knowledge spoken by the spirit in the person that will identify what spirit it is. If it is the Spirit of God with our born-again spirit, then our soul will be transforming by God's wisdom and we will sin less and less as the transformation moves forward. The end results is, we will not be workers of iniquity but those who walk in holiness.

Christ also points out that those with demonic spirits will be able to prophecy (Prophet lie) in Christ's name, seem to cast out devils, and do wonderful works. Yet the person will still be walking in wickedness because no transformation will be taking place. This does not change the fact that what Christ means by fruits of the corrupt tree, which He identifies as trees of thorns and thistles, are the fruit of their lips. Spoken knowledge that is corrupt is their fruit.

Matt 24:4-5

4 And Jesus answered and said unto them, **Take heed that no man deceive you.**

5 For **many shall come in my name, saying, I am Christ; and shall deceive many.**

KJV

Matt 12:34-37

34 **O generation of vipers, how can ye, being evil, speak good things?** For out of the **abundance of the heart the mouth speaketh.**

35 A good man out of the good treasure of the heart bringeth forth good things: and an evil man out of the evil treasure bringeth forth evil things.

36 But I say unto you, **That every idle word that men shall speak, they shall give account thereof in the day of judgment.**

37 For **by thy words thou shalt be justified, and by thy words thou shalt be condemned.**

KJV

The above verse should leave no question of what the fruits are that Christ is speaking about on the corrupt trees. Let me also give you a small gem. Christ was not calling those men vipers He was addressing the spirits in them speaking through them first, then He moved on to addressing the men. Every word that comes through us is first approved by us. We come into agreement with it whether our soul or those taking up residence in us speak it. It does not matter if we know they are there or not. We must be quick to rebuke anything we speak that goes against the Word of God, lest we come into agreement with the enemy of our souls.

I was speaking to a young woman who God was calling to salvation, and she was distraught because of what God showed her concerning her boyfriend. She realized she was in a sinful relationship but was finding it hard to break up with the young man. She explained to me that one night while sleeping in the bed with him, she woke up and looked next to her where he was sleeping but all she saw was a bunch of snakes where his body was laying. A few seconds later, it was his body next to her.

I explained to her that God opened up her eyes and what she saw were the demons in his body. It was a terrifying experience and her face revealed the despair. The next day I was witnessing to a young man. He was very prideful and worldly with tattoos covering his whole upper body. He told me he did not believe in God. I shared with him my testimony on how I was a non-believer and God brought me out of it. A short time after our conversation, I realized that this was the man that was the young woman's boyfriend. He was full of snakes and vipers and I could feel the demonic presence as we spoke.

The sad part is that he is not unique. If God would open up the eyes of the world and show them what is living in them, shrieks and screams would fill up the whole atmosphere of the planet. Many people would seriously lose their minds. Sin is an access point to our bodies for demons. If you are full of sin, bet your bottom dollar that you are full of demons. When Christ addressed those men as a generation of vipers, he knew what was in them.

Earlier we discussed when Satan entered Job's wife; we saw that neither she nor Job was aware of it. In the same manner when he entered Judas who betrayed Christ, the disciples were oblivious to it. However, if you paid attention to the things Judas was speaking you would know exactly what gave Satan an opening to enter him. Even the fruit of Peter's mouth revealed the presence of Satan who the Lord quickly rebuked.

If you pay attention to the words coming out of a person's mouth with knowledge of the Word of God and a little experience, you will be able to tell the exact spirit that is speaking. Pride, hate, covetousness, envy, jealousy, lust, and others will always identify themselves; you just have to listen closely. The abundance of the heart is exposed by what the mouth speaks. **The fruit of the lips will always identify what tree (spirit) they came from.** For a deeper understanding of this topic please read the chapter, "Guarding the Door of Our Mouth," in my book "Assault on Innocence."

Christians need to pay close attention to what they hear coming out of people's mouths, it will identify if there is a demonic presence. Evil spirits will always speak contrary to the knowledge of the Kingdom. The more you know of the Kingdom, the easier it becomes to tell what spirit is speaking. When I was a babe in Christ, I loved watching TV evangelists. I would look in awe as they gave those powerful charismatic messages. As I grew spiritually and learned Kingdom knowledge, I started noticing that some of the messages were not lining up with scripture. The more I grew in the knowledge of God the more amazed I was at what I heard coming out of some of their mouths. I even heard a minister tell the congregation the exact message from the serpent, that self can be god. He then had the congregation repeat it after him. By them repeating the words, they were signing a covenant with their mouths. They just sat there oblivious to what he was doing. This is another example of why the talent (knowledge of the Kingdom) is so important, and how it is a shield of protection.

The curse fell on Adam and through him, all humankind died spiritually. The curse cannot be lifted until you come to Christ. Adam's spirit was dead (in a state of separation), and he had no access to the things of the spirit. The spirit realm became dark to him. In the sense of the spiritual, he was walking as a blind man. **Adam had so much potential for natural and spiritual life, if only he had made the right choice and eaten from the tree of life (spoken to the right angel).** Everyone died with his spiritual death, and then God reminded him and us that in that sinful state, all we have to look forward to is returning to the dust we were taken from. No hope for the wicked, dust returns to dust. However, for those who put their hope in Christ, Adam's curse is dissolved. We have hope in Christ Jesus for eternal life for all who endure to the end.

Chapter 10

The Serpent's tale

Gen 3:14-15

14 And the LORD God said unto the serpent , Because thou hast done this, thou art cursed above all cattle, and above every beast of the field; **upon thy belly** shalt thou go, and **dust shalt thou eat all the days of thy life:**

15 And I will put **enmity between thee and the woman, and between thy seed and her seed; it shall bruise thy head, and thou shalt bruise his heel.**

KJV

So many believe that the serpent was a talking snake, they are lost in the metaphor. Did you notice that nowhere in the curse did God remove the serpent's speech? If it were a talking snake, then snakes would still be able to talk today. Sometimes we look past the obvious. As I showed earlier, the serpent was actually the Devil who was a Cherub angel disguised as a seraphim messenger angel to deceive Eve.

Always pay attention to when God hands out curses and judgments because they will always be specific to the sin and the person. The penalty will identify aspects of the person or the crime. With the parable of the talents, the wicked servant said the master picks up what he did not lay down and reaps what he did not sow. The master took the talent from the servant and gave it to the one who had the most who did not lay it down or sow it. Eve was cursed in childbirth, which was her purpose. Her very name meaning mother of all living. Adam's curse reflected his purpose as a gardener. God cursed the ground so it would not produce its fullness. The curse also included what was sown in his own heart.

The serpent was cursed to go on his belly. I have heard it preached that snakes had legs. Where does it say the serpent had legs? Once again, lost in the metaphor!

Satan was cursed to go on his belly but he is not a snake, so we need to understand what the metaphor for belly really means. The Hebrew word translated belly is "*gachown*," which literally means the abdomen region of the body. This Hebrew word is only utilized twice in scripture, both times in Genesis for animals that creep, and for Satan as the serpent. Other words are also utilized for belly and also as a metaphor. Let's look at some of them as we go forward on this pathway of understanding:

Job 15:35
35 They conceive mischief, and bring forth vanity, and their **belly** prepareth deceit.
KJV

How does a person's belly prepare deceit? Can your stomach think? The belly is a metaphor for the soul or mind, also called the heart in scripture, and it points to the carnal nature. When we think of belly, we think of food to satisfy the flesh. This is as if the carnal minded man is drawn towards things to satisfy self.

Ps 44:25
25 For our **soul is bowed down to the dust: our belly cleaveth unto the earth.**
KJV

If you take the time to read the whole chapter, you will see that judgment has fallen on Israel even though the writer is not sure what the cause is. They are humbled and oppressed because of judgment. And once again, the belly is the soul:

Prov 18:8
8 The words of a talebearer are as wounds, and they go down into the innermost parts of the belly.
KJV

When people speak wickedness against you it cuts to the soul. Again, the belly is representing the soul.

Prov 20:27
27 The spirit of man is the candle of the LORD, searching all the inward parts of the belly.
KJV

God's candle is not searching to see what you have eaten carnally. He is searching to see what you have ingested into your soul, identifying what is in you.

Now pay close attention to this, read it twice if you have to, because this identifies Satan's issue, which we are going to shine the light on:

Phil 3:18-19
18(For many walk, of whom I have told you often, and now tell you even weeping, that they are the enemies of the cross of Christ:
19 Whose end is destruction, **whose God is their belly, and whose glory is in their shame, who mind earthly things.)**
KJV

Did you see that? Their god is their belly. Carnal soul has become their god. **They mind earthly things** that will satisfy the flesh. Their mindset is on the stuff and the abundance of things. They are more concerned with the carnal than with the spiritual because the carnal satisfies the flesh, which is a carnal mind ruling them as their god. Carnal-minded Christians.

Ok, I need you to take a short break and get a snack, a refreshing drink, and take a deep breath. You're going to need some air because we are about to go into some deep waters. Don't worry you know I will be right here when you get back.

Stop cheating!

Ok, are you ready? Let's dive. I want you to read this carefully and slowly:

Ezek 28:13-16

13 Thou hast been in Eden the garden of God; every precious stone was thy covering, the sardius, topaz, and the diamond, the beryl, the onyx, and the jasper, the sapphire, the emerald, and the carbuncle, and gold: the workmanship of thy tabrets and of thy pipes was prepared in thee in the day that thou wast created.

14 Thou art the anointed cherub that covereth; and I have set thee so: thou wast upon the holy mountain of God; thou hast walked up and down in the midst of the stones of fire.

15 Thou wast perfect in thy ways from the day that thou wast created, till iniquity was found in thee.

16 By **the multitude of thy merchandise they have filled the midst of thee with violence, and thou hast sinned**: therefore I will cast thee as profane out of the mountain of God: and I will destroy thee, O covering cherub, from the midst of the stones of fire.

KJV

I am not going to break it all down, because we went over it with the discussion on the tree being Satan. I just wanted you to read the whole thing to bring you to the understanding that Satan had a lot of stuff. God blessed him from his creation, and it got to his head. **The multitude of thy merchandise was the issue**, not because he received it but because he allowed it to corrupt his heart (midst of thee). Satan wanted more, and his eyes even fell upon earthly things. You see that word violence? It is translated from the Hebrew word "*chamac* ," and it means to take unjust gain. The word is often used with robbery. Pay attention to what he uses to try and bribe Christ:

Luke 4:2-8

2 Being forty days tempted of the devil. And in those days he did eat nothing: and when they were ended, he afterward hungered.

3 And the devil said unto him, **If thou be the Son of God, command this stone that it be made bread.**

4 And Jesus answered him, saying, **It is written, That man shall not live by bread alone, but by every word of God.**

5 And the devil, taking him up into an high mountain, shewed unto him all the kingdoms of the world in a moment of time.

6 And the devil said unto him, **All this power will I give thee, and the glory of them: for that is delivered unto me; and to whomsoever I will I give it.**

7 If thou therefore wilt worship me, all shall be thine.

8 And Jesus answered and said unto him, **Get thee behind me, Satan: for it is written, Thou shalt worship the Lord thy God, and him only shalt thou serve.**

KJV

The first attack on Christ came at the flesh. Why? Satan is cast down on his belly (carnal mindset) that is what he knows. Remember, it is not just Satan, it is also approximately 50 million other fallen angels (see "Assault on Innocence" for calculations). The curse that fell upon Satan and his kingdom is lust for the merchandise and the things of this world. Don't believe me? Look back at verse 6. Satan is showing off all that he has to Christ. Look at all my stuff! Did you notice that he said it was delivered to him and not given? He stole it from Adam.

Satan used the lust for knowledge, the desire to be more than they were created to be, to entrap Adam and Eve. The curse bound him to the same carnal mindset of the belly (carnal nature) to get more. It's the abundance of things. Look at the discussion below between Christ and Peter who Satan was speaking through at the time. I know some believe it was not the Devil because the word means adversary, so it is taught some places that he was just addressing Peter. This teaching is not correct; it was the Devil speaking through him. You can clearly see this because after Jesus rebukes Satan, who is speaking through Peter, He follows with a teaching about self and things:

Matt 16:21-26

21 From that time forth began Jesus to shew unto his disciples, how that he must go unto Jerusalem, and suffer many things of the elders and chief priests and scribes, and be killed, and be raised again the third day.

22 Then Peter took him, and began to rebuke him, saying, Be it far from thee, Lord: this shall not be unto thee.

23 But he turned, and said unto Peter, Get thee behind me, Satan: thou art an offence unto me: **for thou savourest not the things that be of God, but those that be of men.**

24 Then said Jesus unto his disciples, If any man will come after me, let him deny himself, and take up his cross, and follow me.

25 For whosoever will save his life shall lose it: and whosoever will lose his life for my sake shall find it.

26 For **what is a man profited, if he shall gain the whole world, and lose his own soul? or what shall a man give in exchange for his soul?**

KJV

Christ rebukes the devil, pointing out that he savourest (set affection on) the things of this world and not the things of God. Christ points out that even though Satan has gained the world, he is condemned. He is speaking to Satan and all humankind that would follow after Satan's ways. Peter had an open door of self. It was exposed when he denied Christ because the preservation of self was more important than standing with Christ like John did. The devil identified this mindset in Peter and used it as an entrance point.

Anything negative we say is a open door.

Many years ago, I had a vision of looking down a long hallway. To the right and left of me were doors. It reminded me of a floor in a hotel with multiple doors. All of a sudden, I saw a person walking but all I could see was their feet, which were green with scales like a reptile. As he got to each door, I would see a hand reach up turning the doorknob to see if the door would open. The door was locked and he would move on to the next door. I realized it was a demon, and then the Holy Spirit revealed that Satan was looking for an open door into my life. He was looking for an entrance to get in and fight me from the inside. Satan was looking for something from his kingdom that he had authority over that was in me, and could be used as a weapon against me. As the vision was ending, I gasped as the scaly green hand turned a knob and the door opened.

As a babe in Christ, I was still in that stage of carnality and through my flesh and carnal mind, the enemy found an opening. It took many years with hard lessons as the Holy Spirit taught me how to secure the door. Even after I learned how to secure it, I still had to learn how to keep it secured.

Jesus went through this same scenario and proclaimed that even though Satan was coming he had no entrance point, no unsecured doors. Satan had nothing in Christ to give him entrance:

John 14:30
30 Hereafter I will not talk much with you: for **the prince of this world cometh, and hath nothing in me.**
KJV

Peter and the other disciples had the same struggles and fell many times, as they learned to surrender this carnal nature. Do you realize that Christ had to intercede twice in a dispute among the disciples on who would be the greatest? This is walking in Satan's territory of pride. That exposed the carnal mindset that Christ reproved (corrected) to by saying the greatest is like a child and a servant. Peter can be identified as a main party in those disputes by his actions in questioning Christ about John after Christ prophesied of how Peter's life would end. Peter wanted to compare John's ending to his own.

John 21:18-22
18 Verily, verily, I say unto thee, When thou wast young, thou girdedst thyself, and walkedst whither thou wouldest: but when thou shalt be old, thou shalt stretch forth thy hands, and another shall gird thee, and carry thee whither thou wouldest not.
19 **This spake he, signifying by what death he should glorify God.** And when he had spoken this, he saith unto him, Follow me.
20 Then Peter, turning about, seeth the disciple whom Jesus loved following; which also leaned on his breast at supper, and said, Lord, which is he that betrayeth thee?
21 Peter seeing him saith to Jesus, **Lord, and what shall this man do?**
22 Jesus saith unto him, **If I will that he tarry till I come, what is that to thee?** Follow thou me.
KJV

Again, Peter was given correction. Who teaches like God? We know from church history that when it all came down to it, Peter learned his lessons well. Peter gave his life to glorify God, refusing to be crucified upright like Christ because he deemed himself unworthy.

149

They crucified him upside down a testimony to the glory of God and His power to change the hearts of men. Glory be to God!

Who was the other disciple that the devil entered? Judas! What was the downfall of Judas? The love of money took him down:

John 12:4-6
4 Then saith one of his disciples, Judas Iscariot, Simon's son, which should betray him,
5 Why was not this ointment sold for three hundred pence, and given to the poor?
6 This he said, not that he cared for the poor; but because **he was a thief , and had the bag, and bare what was put therein.**
KJV

We can fill another book with those who have been bound by Satan to covet (lust) for things, the pride of the abundance of things, and power. **The love of money root develops from the seed of covetousness because money enables those who lust to get the abundance of things.**

Luke 12:15
15 And he said unto them, **Take heed, and beware of covetousness: for a man's life consisteth not in the abundance of the things** which he possesseth.
KJV

Many years I have prayed for understanding concerning a description from the book of Revelation. Christ mentions in His messages to the churches, **the synagogue of Satan.** He mentions it twice when speaking to the churches of Philadelphia and Smyrna. I want you to read these scriptures and think about what He is saying:

Rev 2:9
9 I know thy works, and tribulation, and **poverty, (but thou art rich)** and I know the blasphemy of them which say they are Jews, and are not, but are **the synagogue of Satan.**
KJV

Rev 3:8-9

8 I know thy works: behold, I have set before thee an open door, and no man can shut it: for thou hast **a little strength**, and hast kept my word, and hast not denied my name.

9 Behold, **I will make them of the synagogue of Satan**, which say they are Jews, and are not, but do lie; behold, I will make them to come and worship before thy feet, and to know that I have loved thee.

KJV

I realized that the churches had **"little strength" and "poverty."** These were the only two churches mentioned in Revelation that Christ found no fault with. These are also the only two churches that He mentioned with the synagogues of Satan. Christ paints a picture of them being in direct conflict with the synagogues of Satan. However, why didn't He mention the synagogue of Satan with the other churches?

A synagogue is not what most Christians believe. It is not a church. It can be a small group of men (ten). The focus is on a place of teaching. When Israel went into exile, it was a way of keeping the focus on God's Word. Synagogues were set up as places to teach the Word of God. Throughout the scriptures, you find Christ and many of the disciples entering synagogues to teach or debate the truth of the scriptures. The synagogue of Satan is not Satan's church, it is a place teaching the ideology of Satan. This is why it is in direct conflict with the little church (Philadelphia), and the poverty-stricken church (Smyrna), who just happens to be the perfect churches. Little and poor is in direct conflict with big and rich. The ideology of Satan is the covetous soul wanting the abundance of things. Understanding this is a key. Now watch how it opens another door of understanding to a verse that to me made no sense:

Matt 6:24

24 No man can **serve two masters**: for either he will hate the one, and love the other; or else he will hold to the one, and despise the other. **Ye cannot serve God and mammon.**

KJV

I could not figure out why it says we can't serve God and mammon (wealth/riches). It made no sense to me. I always thought it should read "God and Satan." In my mind, they were the two that were/are in conflict for our souls. I would later realize that Satan is not fighting God because he is not stupid. He knows he can't win. Satan is fighting **us**. His number one weapon is his bellies ideology, which is covetousness and the abundance of things. It is the love of money also known as wealth, which is the definition of mammon.

Rom 16:18
18 For they that are such **serve not our Lord Jesus Christ, but their own belly;** and by **good words and fair speeches deceive the hearts of the simple.**
KJV

Phil 3:18-20
18(For many walk, of whom I have told you often, and now tell you even weeping, that they are the enemies of the cross of Christ:
19 Whose end is destruction, **whose God is their belly,** and whose glory is in their shame, **who mind earthly things.**)
20 For our conversation is in heaven; from whence also we look for the Saviour, the Lord Jesus Christ:
KJV *We are instructed to kill our flesh daily*

Their god is not their stomach it is just a symbolism. Their god or gods are the carnal fleshly nature. They want earthly things to satisfy the flesh. The flesh is the region of the body where Satan and his demons rule. It cannot be redeemed; it can only be put to death. This is why we are instructed to continue the process of killing the flesh daily. When it no longer has influence over the soul because the soul has been transformed, then the flesh is dead.

The attack on the church is in full effect. Rom 16:18 talks about "good words and fair speeches" this is what is presented to the simple by motivational speakers masquerading as pastors. They draw the simple with promises of blessings and abundance and those under the spell of covetousness don't realize they are in the synagogue of Satan laying money at the altar because money has replaced the blood of Jesus at their altars.

Prov 1:29-33

29 For that they hated knowledge, and did not choose the fear of the LORD:

30 They would none of my counsel: they despised all my reproof.

31 Therefore shall **they eat of the fruit of their own way, and be filled with their own devices.**

32 For the turning away of the simple shall slay them, **and the prosperity of fools shall destroy them.**

33 But whoso hearkeneth unto me shall dwell safely, and shall be quiet from fear of evil.

KJV

I want you to understand that the world system that we live in is built and based on the love of money. This mindset rules this present world. The need of the abundance of things is propagated on TV, in the schools, and in the hearts of the people. Sadly, it has even infiltrated many of the Christian churches with a prosperity Gospel, which has replaced the Gospel of peace. Among Christian churches, the love of money is more prevalent than we think and it is spreading. Now I need you to read the scriptures below twice and very carefully:

1 Tim 6:5-12

5 Perverse disputings of men of corrupt minds, and destitute of the truth, **supposing that gain is godliness**: from such withdraw thyself.

6 But **godliness with contentment is great gain.**

7 For **we brought nothing into this world, and it is certain we can carry nothing out.**

8 And having food and raiment let us be therewith content.

9 But **they that will be rich fall into temptation and a snare, and into many foolish and hurtful lusts, which drown men in destruction and perdition.**

10 For **the love of money is the root of all evil: which while some coveted after, they have erred from the faith, and pierced themselves through with many sorrows.**

11 But **thou, O man of God, flee these things; and follow after righteousness, godliness, faith, love, patience, meekness.**

12 Fight the good fight of faith, **lay hold on eternal life**, whereunto thou art also called, and hast professed a good profession before many witnesses.
KJV

What profit a man... You should know the rest and have a better understanding of why Christ said this:

Luke 18:25
25 For it is easier for a camel to go through a needle's eye, **than for a rich man to enter into the kingdom of God.**
KJV

Everything is starting to make sense, don't you think?

Snakes do not eat dirt yet

Sometimes we look so hard into a matter that we overlook the obvious. Snakes do not eat the dust of the ground as of yet. Now I know that scripture says that in the new Kingdom snakes shall eat dust (Isa 65:25). Yet, the curse says the serpent shall eat dust, all his life, and since snakes do not eat dust then this confirms again that the serpent in the Garden was not a snake. The devil and all his fallen angels have the curse that fell on him. Do they feed on dust? Yes, they do. No, they do not eat dirt. Did you ever notice that everything eaten in the natural realm comes from the dust of the ground? There is only one time in the history of this world that people ate something that was not originating from the ground:

Manna, Corn of heaven, angels food

Ps 78:23-25
23 Though he had commanded the clouds from above, and opened the doors of heaven,
24 And had rained down manna upon them to eat, and had given them of **the corn of heaven.**
25 Man did eat angels' food: he sent them meat to the full.

If the fallen angels no longer have access to the food from heaven, then they are eating the food from the earth. Either directly or indirectly, through the bodies that they enter they are feeding on the dust of the ground. *Corn of heaven - blessings of God.*

Two seds

Gen 3:15
15 And I will put enmity between thee and the woman, and between thy seed and her seed; it shall bruise thy head, and thou shalt bruise his heel.
KJV

In the second part of the curse that fell on Satan, God paints a picture of a woman hating (enmity) snakes and of a man stomping on the head of a snake with his heel. Yet again, this dark saying needs to be unraveled. It makes so much sense to the natural understanding, but it becomes a guard against the spiritual understanding. When things seem to make sense in the natural we do not even take the time to look in the spiritual. Women hate snakes so you picture in your mind that fear of snakes, and **you're lead away from the true meaning** of the verse (remember this, you will understand later).

When God goes deep, He goes way beyond our carnal understanding. This part of the curse has nothing to do with Eve. Eve is not the woman. Remember the verse says Satan will hate the woman. I do not want to keep reiterating the fact that this is not a snake, but reiteration can be a good thing sometimes. Is there any proof that snakes hate women? Do you think snakes kill more women than men, at a vastly higher-rate? No! Remember precept on precept, precept on precept, line line, line line. Here a little, there a little. There is a verse in the Bible that will uncover who the woman is that Satan hates. **If we can find that key, then the dark saying will start to unravel.** Sometimes we have to travel a great distance to find a key of knowledge that will open up our understanding. Let's leave the first book of the Bible and jump all the way to the last:

Rev 12:17
17 And **the dragon was wroth with the woman,** and went to make war with the remnant of her seed, which keep the commandments of God, and have the testimony of Jesus Christ.
KJV

Now we see that the dragon hated (wroth) the woman and went to make war against her seed. Yes, I realize it says dragon and not serpent. Before we backtrack to find out just what this familiar dragon was mad about, let's first cement in your mind that this is that crafty cherub angel Satan who disguised himself as a seraphim (serpent) to deceive Eve.

Rev 20:2
2 And he laid hold on **the dragon, that old serpent, which is the Devil, and Satan**, and bound him a thousand years,
KJV

We know that old serpent and the dragon are one and the same. Now let's backtrack to identify the woman, her seed, and the seed of the devil.

The Woman and Her Seed

Rev 12:1
12:1 And there appeared a great wonder in heaven; a woman clothed with the sun, and the moon under her feet, and upon her head a crown of twelve stars:
KJV

I remember reading a prophecy book years ago where the author gave a handful of interpretations to identify who this woman is. There were so many different people identified because everyone was coming up with private interpretation instead of letting the scriptures identify her. When I look at this I don't try to figure out who this is, I just try to find the scripture that tells me who she is. Let's head on back to Genesis. Here we find Joseph telling his family about a dream that he dreamed. Pay attention to Jacob's (his father) response to him.

Gen 37:9-10
9 And he dreamed yet another dream, and told it his brethren, and said, Behold, I have dreamed a dream more; and, behold, **the sun and the moon and the eleven stars made obeisance to me.**

10 And he told it to his father, and to his brethren: and his father rebuked him, and said unto him, What is this dream that thou hast dreamed? **Shall I and thy mother and thy brethren** indeed come to bow down ourselves to thee to the earth?
KJV

Jacob identifies the sun as himself and the moon as his wife. Joseph saw eleven stars while John described the woman with 12 stars on her head. Why is there a difference? Joseph was one of the twelve stars and he did not see himself because it was from his viewpoint. The twelve stars are Joseph and his brothers. The woman is the tribe of Israel, which seed will be personified through Mary. The seed she gives birth to is the same seed that came through Israel and it is Christ the Lord Jesus (Yehoshua/God's salvation). This is the woman that gave birth to the seed that the devil wanted so desperately to kill. (For a deeper breakdown of Rev 12, please see "Assault on Innocence".)

Now that we have identified the woman, we also realize that Christ is the child. The description of the child makes identification obvious:

Rev 12:5
5 And she brought forth a man child, who was to **rule all nations** with a rod of iron: and **her child was caught up unto God, and to his throne.** Israel- her   nations- people

Satan hated Israel and went to make war against her, but God hid her away in the wilderness. When the Bible uses "hiding in the wilderness" as a metaphor, it is speaking of among the nations of the world. Think about it, for almost two thousand years there were literally dozens (or more) groups around the world claiming to be the lost tribes of Israel. They are lost to men but God knows exactly where and who they are and when He will gather them all back together. He also knows all those who make up spiritual Israel by being members of the Body of Christ who are identified by having the Holy Spirit. Natural Israel was never lost, just hidden away as Rev 12 says. Do you realize that the Bible actually names the places where God hid Israel? Another time another place.

Satan tries to kill Christ the child that was born but is unable to because He is the Son of God. Resurrection ruined the enemy's plans while fulfilling exactly what God said He would do. Therefore, the deathblow to Christ was nothing more than a strike on his heel. What is so powerful about the prophecy of Genesis, concerning wounding the seed's heel, is that recent archeological finds prove the prophecy in the natural sense. Jesus was nailed from the side of the foot in both heels to the tree. It was not in the front behind the toes as shown in most depictions. Each heel was on the sides of the post and the nails were driven in through the sides. Prophecy fulfilled in the spiritual and natural.

We have to understand that all believers are of the Body of Christ. In the spiritual, we are the bride of Christ and are joined to Him becoming one spiritual body:

Eph 5:30-32
30 For **we are members of his body** , of his flesh, and of his bones.
31 For this cause shall a man leave his father and mother, and shall be joined unto his wife, and they two shall be one flesh.
32 **This is a great mystery: but I speak concerning Christ and the church.** KJV

What this means is that we become the seed with Christ and are grafted into spiritual Israel. That is why the Devil proceeds to attack us, the remnant of her seed. I want you to understand this; the woman is Israel the seed is who Israel gave birth to. The nation of Israel cannot be both Israel and her seed. The unbelieving Jews and those lost tribes are the woman. The remnant of her seed that the scripture is talking about, who have the testimony of Jesus Christ and keep the commandments of God, are those who are baptized into the Body of Christ. They also keep the commandments brought by Christ, which He stated was given to Him from the Father. Therefore, those who teach that the scripture is talking about those who keep the Law of Moses are the seed, are not correct. The testimony is the New Covenant under Christ, and the bylaws are everything Christ said to do and everything He said not to do. If you have His Spirit and are walking according to His doctrine, then you are the seed. The Word of God placed in your heart is the seed of Christ growing within you.

158

Rom 16:20

20 And the God of peace shall bruise Satan under your feet
shortly. The grace of our Lord Jesus Christ be with you. Amen.
KJV

Satan's Seed

I do not want to go into a detailed teaching on who Satan's
seed is because I do not have the space. It would take another book
for me to explain in detail. I want to give you enough to make it very
plain to you. **Let me reiterate, a seed is something you plant in
something, and it grows until it has fully reproduced the source
that it was taken from.** The dirt the spiritual seed is planted in is
the soil of your soul. Your soul conforms to any spirit that is planted
in it. The Bible says that the Word of God is spirit and it is life.
Well, Satan's word is spirit and it is death. Whichever one you ingest
and obey is going to manifest life or death. You are what you eat.
Those who have ingested words of death from Satan and walk in
obedience to it become his spiritual children. Satan and his kingdom
have full access to all his children. If you have embraced and are
walking in unrighteousness, which is contrary to God's will, then no
matter what the degree, you are the child of the devil:

John 8:44

44 Ye are of your father the devil, and **the lusts of your father ye
will do.** He was a murderer from the beginning, and abode not in
the truth, because there is no truth in him. When he speaketh a lie, he
speaketh of his own: for he is a liar, and the father of it.
KJV

1 John 3:10

10 In this the children of God are manifest, and the children of the
devil: whosoever doeth not righteousness is not of God, neither he
that loveth not his brother.
KJV

Just as the devil tempted and persecuted Christ, his children
will follow suit. Remember that just as the Holy Spirit is living in us,
there will be a demonic spirit abiding in Satan's seed (children).
Sometimes they are completely oblivious to this because they are

spiritually blind and do not realize they are a vessel for demons. Other times they will know full well and be in league with the demon, calling it their spirit guide or their ancestral spirit. Don't you be fooled; it is a demon taking up occupancy in a child of Satan. They persecuted Christ so you can bet your bottom dollar that they will also look for every opportunity to oppose and persecute you. Scripture confirms this:

Acts 13:8-11

8 But **Elymas the sorcerer (for so is his name by interpretation) withstood them, seeking to turn away the deputy from the faith.**
9 Then Saul, (who also is called Paul,) filled with the Holy Ghost, set his eyes on him,
10 And said, **O full of all subtilty and all mischief, thou child of the devil, thou enemy of all righteousness, wilt thou not cease to pervert the right ways of the Lord?**
11 And now, behold, the hand of the Lord is upon thee, and thou shalt be blind, not seeing the sun for a season. And immediately there fell on him a mist and a darkness; and he went about seeking some to lead him by the hand.
KJV

Expect the fight. Look for it because it will surely come. When we understand this, then we will not be caught off guard. We will prepare ourselves **on a daily basis** for the fight that will come against us from Satan's seed and the forces of evil. When we do not, we will fall on a daily basis. Be prepared for war because the battles are raging all around us.

God has ensured us that through Christ we will bruise the head of the enemy. Let's make no mistake that Christ has crushed the head of the enemy. His death and resurrection has freed from death all those who believe.

Heb 2:14

14 Forasmuch then as the children are partakers of flesh and blood, he also himself likewise took part of the same; that **through death he might destroy him that had the power of death, that is, the devil;**
KJV

Satan and his kingdom no longer have dominion over us who walk according to the will of God. Satan and all his angels are cast down to the earth and are awaiting final judgment. He is raging because he knows that his time is short. We might think that it is taking a while, but for angels that might have been alive for multiple billions of years or longer, two thousand years is like a grain of sand compared to all the worlds' beaches. He knows his time is getting shorter and shorter each day, and he is in a rage to destroy as many as he can:

Rev 12:12

12 Therefore rejoice, ye heavens, and ye that dwell in them. **Woe to the inhabiters of the earth and of the sea! for the devil is come down unto you, having great wrath, because he knoweth that he hath but a short time.**
KJV

Adam and Eve became victims in the war that Satan was raging against them. We cannot even say they were the first victims because scripture reveals that one third of the angels fell also, all of them bond up in covetousness. It is funny how sometimes we cannot see what we have **because our head is down complaining about what we do not have.** Everyone wants more than what they have, not realizing God has given us everything that we need.

The angels have access to the universe. They have seen things that will make us gasp. Wonders beyond our understanding, in this realm and the spirit realm. These are beings that have gazed upon the wonders of heaven and stood in the presence of God's throne. Yet they wanted more and followed a lustful, covetous entity that wanted it all for himself. In the end, they lost everything that they had.

I have been there where I had more than I needed and tried to get more and lost all I had. That's the trick of covetousness, it will convince you that what you have is not enough and draw you to bet it all to get more and in the end, you stand with empty hands.

This covetousness is the reason why so many entertainers, sports' figures, and lottery winners are soon found penniless. Yet the worst of them cannot be compared to the angels that bet all they had believing the king of all liars. They wanted more and followed a lustful, covetous entity that wanted it all. In the end, they lost everything they had.

FALLEN ANGELS SONG

I lift my tired and feeble eyes
To gaze toward the eastern skies
Appearing out of cloud and flame
They come to hear my tale of shame

On this bleak and endless ground
Men have come a witness found
With memories of such dreadful wrong
Six thousand years can stretch so long

On their face a ghostly gaze
And... a question of amaze
Eternal being who cannot die
Yet tear drops dripping from his eyes
So you ask...

What could make an angel cry?
They believed the words of he who lies
He who was favored in God's sight
Uplifted darkness to tread down light....

Thoughts of ascending congregations' hill
Manifest in words... I will I will
So high the price so great the cost
A twinkling of an eye...all lost

You've read the text of legends told
How sons of God became so bold
So hear the tale that I must tell
Of how the fire and brimstone fell

With our glorious horizon bright
We cursed our God and blessed our might
We questioned God of how and why
And raised clenched fist to yonder sky

Our pride took fuel as bread takes leaven
Scholars wrote...THERE WAS WAR IN HEAVEN
We discarded love and embraced hate
At destiny's end...we sealed our fate...

The sword of God in hand of Son
Battle swift....war was done
Now...
While men enter heaven's gate
For eternal fire........
      I sit............
         I wait...........

Little children, young men, and fathers

Adam and Eve exchanged their God-given home and their dominion over this world for a ticket out of the Garden and lost fellowship with God, with a bonus prize of animal skins. **In the end, covetousness leaves us with nothing, worth nothing.** When you embrace the type of thinking that you can have it all, in the end you exchange everything for nothing. Thank God for His mercy because unlike the fallen angels, we have hope in Christ Jesus.

Gen 3:20-21
20 And Adam called his wife's name Eve; because she was the mother of all living.
21 Unto Adam also and to his wife did the LORD God make coats of skins, and clothed them. KJV

Thank God That He Had a Redemption Plan

Rev 3:17-22
17 Because **thou sayest, I am rich, and increased with goods, and have need of nothing**; and knowest not that **thou art wretched, and miserable, and poor, and blind, and naked:**
18 I counsel thee to buy of me gold tried in the fire, that thou mayest be rich; and white raiment, that thou mayest be clothed, and that the shame of thy nakedness do not appear; and anoint thine eyes with eyesalve, that thou mayest see.
19 **As many as I love, I rebuke and chasten: be zealous therefore, and repent.**
20 Behold, I stand at the door, and knock: if any man hear my voice, and open the door, I will come in to him, and will sup with him, and he with me.
21 To him that overcometh will I grant to sit with me in my throne, even as I also overcame, and am set down with my Father in his throne.
22 He that hath an ear, let him hear what the Spirit saith unto the churches. KJV

I understand why Christ said that we must become like children to enter into the Kingdom of heaven. See Adam and Eve were created as spiritual children and they were innocent. Children can see and understand some beautiful things because their minds have not received the level of corruption as the adults of the world. A child will see you crying, come over, pat you, say it will be ok, and give you a hug. Adults will have all types of things racing through their minds before they decide what they should do.

Yet, there are certain things you cannot introduce to children because knowledge of it will overwhelm them, and will cause them harm trying to control something that they have not reached the maturity to handle. In the same way, God keeps things from us spiritual children because He knows that we are not spiritually mature enough to handle it.

This is why spiritual babes in Christ speak in tongues, not knowing what is communicated between their spirit and God. As we grow spiritually, we start operating more in prophecy yet God will speak through us just what He knows that we can handle. Mature Christians will get words of knowledge where we just know. As we mature, we can be trusted with more.

Gen 3:22
22 And the LORD God said, Behold, the man is become as one of us, to know good and evil: and now, lest he put forth his hand, and take also of the tree of life, and eat, and live for ever:
KJV

This is why God forbade Adam and Eve from speaking to Satan. You ever have that crazy family member that you cannot leave alone with the kids because you do not know what will come out of their mouth? You warn the kids to stay away from Uncle Charlie because he just doesn't have them all. Satan made it look like God was keeping something from them, but the truth is, they were not yet capable of handling the corruption of good and evil knowledge. You do not give immature individuals access to everything. They will push the wrong button and then say, "Oops." You also do not want an immature person with access to dangerous knowledge frozen in that eternal state of being. He is immature but has gained all this knowledge that is dangerous and now you want to give him access to eternal life with such a mindset? You see the danger in letting Adam and Eve stay in the Garden with access to the tree of life? **God had to redeem them first and allow them to spiritually mature before he gave them access to the tree of life.** God has to redeem us. Read this carefully:

1 John 2:12-17
12 I write unto you, **little children, because your sins are forgiven you for his name's sake.**
13 I write unto you, **fathers, because ye have known him that is from the beginning.** I write unto you, **young men, because ye have overcome the wicked one.** I write unto you, **little children, because ye have known the Father.**
14 I have written unto you, **fathers, because ye have known him that is from the beginning.** I have written unto you, **young men, because ye are strong, and the word of God abideth in you, and ye have overcome the wicked one.**
15 Love not the world, neither the things that are in the world. If any man love the world, the love of the Father is not in him.
16 For all that is in the world, the lust of the flesh, and the lust of the eyes, and the pride of life, is not of the Father, but is of the world.
17 And the world passeth away, and the lust thereof: but he that doeth the will of God abideth for ever.
KJV

John is a powerful writer. He has a way of emphasizing a point that if you catch on to what he is saying you get a big smile on your face, because you realize it is the Holy Spirit working heavily through John. Did you notice that the normal procession of things should have been children, young men, and fathers? Instead of the norm, he placed young men last to emphasize a point.

This is the point John is making. Spiritual children attain this level because their sins are forgiven for His name's sake. They have come to know the Father. Children grow into spiritual young men when they overcome the wicked one. They do this by becoming strong by allowing the Word of God to abide in them, which is how they overcome the wicked one. Young men then become spiritual fathers when they know Him that is from the beginning (Christ Jesus). To know Him is to put on his image. This is the process of spiritual growth. Then John emphasizes that separation from the world (in it but not of it) is how we assure our spiritual growth while abiding in God's Word. When we become spiritual fathers, we can be trusted with the knowledge of God. Paul reiterates John's teaching in his own way:

reiterates

1 Cor 13:8-13

8 Charity never faileth: but whether there be prophecies, they shall fail; whether there be tongues, they shall cease; whether there be knowledge, it shall vanish away.

9 For we know in part, and we prophesy in part.

10 But **when that which is perfect is come, then that which is in part shall be done away.**

11 **When I was a child, I spake as a child, I understood as a child, I thought as a child: but when I became a man, I put away childish things.**

12 For now we see through a glass, darkly; but then face to face: now I know in part; but then shall I know even as also I am known.

13 And **now abideth faith, hope, charity, these three; but the greatest of these is charity.**

KJV

When we are children, we still speak like the world, understand like the world (carnal), and think like the world. When we put away the world, which is Satan's kingdom, we put on Christ, which is perfection. The perfection that Paul is talking about is when we reject this world and the things of Satan, the wicked one, and walk in love for each other and love for God. We walk in obedience to Christ's doctrine and have put on Christ. We are no longer babes, and we now know Christ even as He knows us.

I do not want you to get scared by the word "perfection" because the enemy of our souls has done a good job in getting Christians to believe we cannot walk in a sinless lifestyle. Christ would never tell someone to go and sin no more if it was impossible for them to do it. They have implemented a delusion that the bar is so high that it is impossible to attain it, even though scripture emphasizes that we can. Let me bring the bar back down to its proper place by sharing what an old Christian friend shared with me many years ago. Jarvis White said, "Perfection is, what Christ say do, do it and what He say don't do, don't do it." It's as simple as that. I said simple, not easy. Peter shows us that to reach this place comes with much suffering against sin.

1 Peter 4:1-2
4:1 Forasmuch then as Christ hath suffered for us in the flesh, **arm yourselves likewise with the same mind: for he that hath suffered in the flesh hath ceased from sin;**
2 That he **no longer should live the rest of his time in the flesh to the lusts of men, but to the will of God.**
KJV

Paul confirms that this is not a fairy tale but a point that every single born again believer should be striving for. Read slowly:

Titus 2:11-15
11 For the **grace of God** that bringeth salvation hath appeared to all men,
12 **Teaching us** that, denying ungodliness and worldly lusts, we should live soberly, righteously, and godly, **in this present world;**
13 Looking for that blessed hope, and the glorious appearing of the great God and our Saviour Jesus Christ;
14 Who gave himself for us, that he might **redeem us from all iniquity, and purify unto himself a peculiar people, zealous of good works.**
15 These things **speak, and exhort, and rebuke with all authority.** Let no man despise thee.
KJV

Did you notice that it is the **GRACE OF GOD** that teaches us to deny ungodliness and worldly lusts? Did you notice that we are **REQUIRED** to live soberly, righteously, and godly lives? Paul then emphasizes that it is to be done in **THIS PRESENT WORLD.** Paul says we are to speak and exhort this doctrine. Why are so many preaching false doctrine that we have to sin while we are in the flesh and cannot stop until we get to heaven? He also said to rebuke everything that comes against this truth with all authority. It is written, "Greater is He that is in me than he that is in the world." The greater that is in us can overcome the world if we allow Him. Let's not corrupt the truth of God's Word. Take a deep breath we are almost done. I know this has been a long journey, but do you hear all those talents jingling in your bag? In addition, you still have what you came with so the blessings of God are flowing indeed.

Chapter 11

He That Overcomes

Gen 3:23
23 Therefore the LORD God sent him forth from the garden of
Eden, to till the ground from whence he was taken.
KJV

We now have an in-depth understanding of how Adam and
Eve got put out. Here is the new question. How do we get back in,
or even better, where do we enter back in? Christ Himself easily
answers the first part of the question. (I love to use scripture to
answer questions.) When Christ was last seen in the Bible, it was by
John. The Father sent Christ to John with a revelation on what was
to come. Revelation contains directions on how to qualify to enter
back into the Garden of Eden, which is the paradise of God. Christ
gave seven messages to John for the seven churches. Contained in
each message was the word overcome along with what we will
receive if we do. Let's look at the very first overcome message:

Rev 2:7
7 He that hath an ear, let him hear what the Spirit saith unto the
churches; **To him that overcometh will I give to eat of the tree of
life, which is in the midst of the paradise of God.**
KJV

Notice Christ said, "I will give," remember what He said.

I want to list all the seven overcome messages even though I will only
be discussing the one pertaining to the Garden:

Rev 2:11
11 He that hath an ear, let him hear what the Spirit saith unto the churches; **He that overcometh shall not be hurt of the second death.**
KJV

Rev 2:17
17 He that hath an ear, let him hear what the Spirit saith unto the churches; **To him that overcometh will I give to eat of the hidden manna, and will give him a white stone, and in the stone a new name written, which no man knoweth saving he that receiveth it.**
KJV

Rev 2:26-29
26 And **he that overcometh, and keepeth my works unto the end, to him will I give power over the nations:**
27 **And he shall rule them with a rod of iron; as the vessels of a potter shall they be broken to shivers: even as I received of my Father.**
28 **And I will give him the morning star.**
29 He that hath an ear, let him hear what the Spirit saith unto the churches.
KJV

Rev 3:5-6
5 **He that overcometh, the same shall be clothed in white raiment; and I will not blot out his name out of the book of life, but I will confess his name before my Father, and before his angels.**
6 He that hath an ear, let him hear what the Spirit saith unto the churches.
KJV

Rev 3:12-13
12 **Him that overcometh will I make a pillar in the temple of my God, and he shall go no more out: and I will write upon him the name of my God, and the name of the city of my God, which is new Jerusalem, which cometh down out of heaven from my God: and I will write upon him my new name.**

13 He that hath an ear, let him hear what the Spirit saith unto the churches.
KJV

Rev 3:21-22
21 To **him that overcometh will I grant to sit with me in my throne, even as I also overcame, and am set down with my Father in his throne.**
22 He that hath an ear, let him hear what the Spirit saith unto the churches.
KJV

Why do so many believe we don't have to overcome anything because Christ did it all?

Ok, back to "he that overcomes" getting access to the tree of life in Paradise. We know that we must overcome to get back to the tree of life in the Garden. We know it is not a tree but is the other Cherub angel that covers the mercy seat, and he possesses the key to eternal life. I have heard many say that this is Michael the archangel. I have heard others say it is Christ. We know it is not Christ because the angel accompanied Christ, who is the shepherd that dwells between the cherubs. I am not sold on Michael either but I do not have any scripture to confirm either way. What we do know, is that this is one angel that we want to talk to indeed.

Look back at all the promises to those who overcome. Can anyone that reads them honestly say that as Christians it is not necessary for us to overcome the world and the wicked one Satan? We are fighting against him and his kingdom that Christ and the apostles identify as the world. If we take an honest evaluation of this present world we live in, we can come to no other conclusion than that it is wicked. God has bestowed everything upon us that we need to be overcomers. If we believe in Christ's message (all of it) then we will be overcomers and we will attain the promises from God. With Christ, we are well able. Put on the whole armor of God, fight the battle, and win!

1 John 5:1-5

5:1 Whosoever believeth that Jesus is the Christ is born of God: and every one that loveth him that begat loveth him also that is begotten of him.

2 By this we know that we love the children of God, when we love God, and keep his commandments.

3 For this is the love of God, that we keep his commandments: and his commandments are not grievous.

4 For whatsoever is born of God overcometh the world: and this is the victory that overcometh the world, even our faith.

5 Who is he that overcometh the world, but he that believeth that Jesus is the Son of God?

KJV

Get off the sidelines and get into the game. Fight the battle. If you need to learn how to armor up please see "Assault on Innocence" (chapter 8) or the excerpt "The Armor of God." You can find them on Amazon on my author's page with all my books (and excerpts from books). Each book also has a Facebook page with links to them.

Be encouraged! Even though we are still fighting, the war is over. **Christ has won, but we still need to win our individual battles to stand with Him in victory. We still have to overcome.** I promise you if you keep fighting according to Christ and the apostles' teachings, then you will overcome. Be diligent in increasing your talents if you are a born-again believer. If you're not please read the steps to salvation at the end of the book.

No, we are not done. I have one more very important chapter for you. I just wanted to take this time to release some of the tension because I know my books can be heavy with so much information. Just breathe! I know a lot of this is new to you, and many false foundations are being broken down. Just breathe.

To all believers, if you are not where you are supposed to be in Christ, just know that your situation is easily fixed. The devil likes to beat us down and accuse us, even to ourselves to keep us from the solution to all our problems. Prayer does fix things because our High Priest has left us with access to the throne of grace.

Remember:
Heb 4:14-16
14 Seeing then that we have a great high priest, that is passed into the heavens, Jesus the Son of God, let us hold fast our profession.
15 For **we have not an high priest which cannot be touched with the feeling of our infirmities; but was in all points tempted like as we are, yet without sin.**
16 Let us therefore come **boldly** unto the throne of grace, that we may obtain mercy, and find grace to help in time of need.
KJV

      I cannot count how many times I have been there. God has never turned me away. I have found mercy and grace there at the mercy seat, which is the throne of grace. Israel's high priest was warned that he could not enter the Holy of Holies anytime he wanted, but only at the set times given to him by God. **Christ has given us believers access so we can enter in anytime we have the need.** The Veil is taken away. It is an open door policy ratified by the blood of Christ. Learn the proper way to enter in (see Assault on Innocence) and go boldly in. **Our High Priest and the Father are waiting with overflowing mercy and grace in your time of need.**

Heb 9:1-5
9:1 Then verily the first covenant had also ordinances of divine service, and a worldly sanctuary.
2 For there was a tabernacle made; the first, wherein was the candlestick, and the table, and the shewbread; which is called the sanctuary.
3 And after the second veil, the tabernacle which is called the Holiest of all;
4 Which had the golden censer, and the ark of the covenant overlaid round about with gold, wherein was the golden pot that had manna, and Aaron's rod that budded, and the tables of the covenant;
5 And over it the cherubims of glory shadowing the mercyseat; of **which we cannot now speak particularly.**
KJV

God has released the understanding so this can now be spoken openly.

John 11:40

5·8·19

Chapter 12

Where Is Your Mercy?

Ex 25:17-22

17 And thou shalt make a mercy seat of pure gold: two cubits and a half shall be the length thereof, and a cubit and a half the breadth thereof.

18 And thou shalt make **two cherubims** of gold, of beaten work shalt thou make them, in the two ends of the mercy seat.

19 And make one cherub on the one end, and the other cherub on the other end: even of the mercy seat shall ye make the cherubims on the two ends thereof.

20 And the cherubims shall stretch forth their wings on high, covering the mercy seat with their wings, and their faces shall look one to another; toward the mercy seat shall the faces of the cherubims be.

21 And thou shalt put the mercy seat above upon the ark; and **in the ark thou shalt put the testimony** that I shall give thee.

22 And there **I will meet with thee, and I will commune with thee from above the mercy seat**, from between the two cherubims which are upon the ark of the testimony, of all things which I will give thee in commandment unto the children of Israel.

KJV

I entered into the dormitory and found Sergeant Joanna Byrd shaken. Sergeant Byrd is one of my sisters in Christ whose fellowship meant a lot to me as a young Christian. It appeared as if she had drifted off and was awakening from sleep, and this was something I can testify that she never did on the job. I did not know

177

what was wrong but her eyes were watery, and she was shaken. She went to the bathroom, and we continued with the night duties

It was a while before she told me what happened; I had forgotten about that night. A couple days after I saw her shaken she said she wanted to share an experience with me. I could see the sadness on her face as she revealed to me what I knew was a vision. She explained how one night she was sitting there in the sergeant's chair, and all of a sudden, this heavy sleepiness came over her out of nowhere. Suddenly, she was out. The next thing she knew she was standing at the east end of the road leading to the institution, 41st street, which was the only entrance to the prison where we worked. She said that as she looked towards the prison all she saw was fire. Fire was everywhere. Everything was ablaze, just burning. It looked to her like the whole world was on fire. She cried out to God with tearful eyes and said, "God where is your mercy?" Then God spoke back and said, "My mercy is at the gate." Sergeant Byrd then told me she heard the buzzer for the front gate go off and it woke her up out of the vision. There was someone standing at the gate.

All I can remember saying was "wow." The vision blew me away. I knew that for God to show her this it must be very important. (I had no idea how important it really was and it would be years before God would give me the revelation of what He was saying.)

There was a moment of silence followed by small talk, and I turned to leave. Then she said something that shocked me. She said, "Sergeant Williams, do you know who was at the gate ringing the buzzer?" I said, "No. Who?" She said, "It was you, you were standing at the gate ringing the buzzer." I said, sighfully, that I could understand because God brought me back from a backslidden state, and I knew it was only because of His mercy. I walked out with a feeling of gratefulness, because of God's mercy, yet saddened because of the reminder of the years of letting Him down. Yet I had it all wrong, and it would be more than 15 years before God would reveal to me what He was really saying.

Gen 3:24

24 So he drove out the man; and he placed at the east of the garden of Eden **Cherubims**, and **a flaming sword** which **turned every way, to keep the way of the tree of life.**
KJV

God was not telling us that He had mercy on me even though it was evident that He did for me to be here writing this. He was letting us know that I was going to be the one He would use to release to the world that the mercy seat is the entrance to the Garden of Eden. **The only way into the Garden is through the mercy seat.**

The cloud

It was July 20, 2017. I walked outside of my home to check on a table I had set up to sell mangoes from my backyard. I exited the porch with my dog Fluff close behind me. I looked up and saw a cloud. What was peculiar about the cloud was that there was a missing portion in the shape of a perfect arrow on the front side pointing back into the middle of the cloud. I stopped and gazed because the arrow looked like someone took a ruler and drew it. It was perfect. Now I have seen a lot of things in my life, and many things from God, so it really takes a lot to surprise me. I was not surprised; I just thought it was peculiar.

I went back inside and a few minutes later, I came back out to find the arrow still there. I then noticed a capital "I" that closely resembled a sideways capital H sitting in the middle of the cloud and the arrow was pointing right at it. This is when I realized that something spiritual was going on. I had just gotten off the phone with one of my Bible students, and my phone went dead. I had placed it on the charger so I had nothing to take a picture of the cloud.

I continued to watch the cloud to see if there was anything else going on, and I noticed it had an orange glare from the sun that was going down because it was late in the evening. The cloud was just glowing. As I kept looking, I noticed something that either I missed or that just appeared. There was the design of feathers like a bird's wing stretched out at the top corner of the cloud. I had no doubt that something spiritual was taking place but from my experience over the years, I knew not to just take it and run with it, saying it was a message from God.

I took off my sandals, knelt down on my knees, spread my arms toward the heavens with head bowed (correct praying position), and prayed to God that if this was from Him to give me the revelation on it and if it was not, then to remove it from my memory. I got up, it was still there, and I watched it for a while then entered my home to digest it while looking through scriptures. The Holy Spirit led me here:

Lev 16:2
2 And the LORD said unto Moses, Speak unto Aaron thy brother, that he come not at all times into the holy place within the vail before the mercy seat, which is upon the ark; that he die not: for **I will appear in the cloud upon the mercy seat.**
KJV

Once I read the scripture, I realized the cloud was confirmation of this book that I had already started writing, which contained the revelation on the two trees in the Garden being the two cherubim that covered the mercy seat. It was God's way of encouraging me and giving me confirmation on what He was showing me.

When the high priest entered the Holy of Holies, he would see an orange glow in the room because God appeared as a fire between the two cherubim. This is what scripture means when it says our God is a consuming fire:

Ex 24:17-18
17 And the sight of the glory of the LORD was like devouring fire on the top of the mount in the eyes of the children of Israel.
18 And Moses went into the midst of the cloud, and gat him up into the mount: and Moses was in the mount forty days and forty nights.
KJV

In the Holy of Holies, the high priest would also carry a censer, which produced smoke to fill the room, concealing God's glory:

Lev 16:12-13

12 And he shall take a censer full of burning coals of fire from off the altar before the LORD, and his hands full of sweet incense beaten small, and bring it within the vail:

13 And he shall put the incense upon the fire before the LORD, that the cloud of the incense may cover the mercy seat that is upon the testimony, that he die not:

KJV

God was not done confirming the revelations for the book.

The Angel, Satan, and the Mango Tree

I do most of my writing sitting on my couch and sometimes this can go long into the night. This particular night I was breaking down the revelation on Satan being one of the two trees in the Garden. Specifically, I was revealing the fact that he was the tree of the knowledge of good and evil. Sleepiness came over me, which I am familiar with, and I knew I was going into a vision. I drifted off lightly and went into the vision. I saw the front yard outside and there were two men standing by my potted plants looking down at them. I saw a man dressed in a white glowing gown-like garment and another man dressed in black pants and a red shirt. The man in white was bent over looking at a specific pot, and it appeared as if he pulled some weeds out of the pot. I secured the vision in my mind and fell asleep.

When I woke up in the morning, the vision came back to me and I got up and went outside. I found the spot where I saw the men standing and the pot I saw the man in white looking at. It was a pot that I had weeded out and planted a mango seedling in. I was shocked to realize that the seedling did something I have never seen a mango seedling do at such a young stage. It split in three with the two end branches opening up leaves that covered the middle stem. It reminded me of the two cherubims on the mercy seat. I ran inside, got my phone, and took a picture of the seedling. This is when I noticed that one of the two end branches had leaves of different colors. It seemed like God wanted me to understand they represented the two men I saw in the vision, representing Satan and the other angel that covered the mercy seat. Again, God was giving me a miraculous confirmation to go along with the scriptures to support the Biblical revelation. Who teaches like God?

Sidenote: The picture of the mango seedling is located on the back of the book. Please take time to look up the Facebook page "Hidden in The Garden" where I have also posted the picture. By clicking like, you can receive other information on the book and other books I have written or will be writing. Feel free to ask any questions or post topics for discussion.

Procrastination

Just a few days from starting these last chapters, I went through a struggle with many spiritual attacks. It felt overwhelming, and I went into prayer. While petitioning God on an understanding of what was happening I heard, "Finish the book." When God gives me a word it is often a small statement with a lot of information attached to it. I tested the spirit by asking the spirit that spoke to me to confess if Jesus Christ (Yehoshua) is the Word of God that came forth from God, dwelled in the flesh and He is the Christ. The spirit confessed, and then repeated, "Finish the book."

The information I received is that I was procrastinating and taking care of other things that the book had priority over and it was important that I finish the book. As I got back to the task, the revelations poured in and I understood how important this book was going to be for the spiritual growth of the believer. That is why the attacks were coming so strong. As you are reading this today, know that it was/is important to God, not just for the powerful revelations that are given. There is something going on in the spirit realm. Those who are close to God can feel the birth pangs of this world. **God is about to do something that requires His people to get a deeper understanding of the Kingdom.** Take a stretch and let's finish this book.

Gen 3:24
24 So he drove out the man; and he placed at the east of the garden of Eden Cherubims, and **a flaming sword** which turned every way, to keep the way of the tree of life.
KJV

God placed the Garden in the east of Eden. When He sent Adam and Eve out they were sent to the east. When He sent Cain into exile, he was sent to the east. When God brings locust, famine, storms, and other negative things, they are often accompanied by an East wind.

Job 15:2
2 Should a wise man utter vain knowledge, and fill his belly with the east wind?
KJV

The east is often a sign of something negative. Are we surprised that the high priest is told to put the blood of the sacrifice at the east end of the mercy seat? Even when he enters into the Holy of Holies, the high priest is walking from the east. God placed at the east of the Garden cherubims and a flaming sword to guard the way to the tree of life. When they tell you to go east turn around and go west, because you will only find problems and deception if you are heading to the spiritual east. The east is where Satan abodes and the east wind is destruction:

Ezek 19:12-13
12 But she was plucked up in fury, she was cast down to the ground, and the east wind dried up her fruit: her strong rods were broken and withered; the fire consumed them.
13 And now she is planted in the wilderness, in a dry and thirsty ground.
KJV

Here is the misconception that many have. When you hear cherubims and a flaming sword, you think of an angel holding up a sword made out of fire. Yet, nowhere in the verse does it say the angels are holding the sword. Moreover, nowhere in scripture will you find an angel holding a flaming sword. The cherubs are not holding the flaming sword. Only one person in scripture is described with a sword of fire. Take the string, tie the precepts together, and let us see what is revealed:

Isa 66:16
16 For **by fire and by his sword** will the LORD plead with all flesh: and the slain of the LORD shall be many.
KJV

Tophet

Isa 30:33
33 For Tophet is ordained of old; yea, for the king it is prepared; he hath made it deep and large: the pile thereof is fire and much wood; **the breath of the LORD, like a stream of brimstone,** doth kindle it.
KJV

Isa 11:4
4 But with righteousness shall he judge the poor, and reprove with equity for the meek of the earth: and **he shall smite the earth with the rod of his mouth, and with the breath of his lips shall he slay the wicked.**
KJV

Rev 19:15-16
15 And **out of his mouth goeth a sharp sword, that with it he should smite the nations:** and he shall rule them with a rod of iron: and he treadeth the winepress of the fierceness and wrath of Almighty God.
16 And he hath on his vesture and on his thigh a name written, KING OF KINGS, AND LORD OF LORDS.
KJV

Isa 30:27-28
27 Behold, the name of the LORD cometh from far, burning with his anger, and the burden thereof is heavy: his lips are full of indignation, and **his tongue as a devouring fire:**
28 And his breath, as an overflowing stream, shall reach to the midst of the neck, to sift the nations with the sieve of vanity: and there shall be a bridle in the jaws of the people, causing them to err.
KJV

2 Thess 2:8
8 And then shall that Wicked be revealed, whom **the Lord shall consume with the spirit of his mouth**, and shall destroy with the brightness of his coming:
KJV

Rev 1:16
16 And he had in his right hand seven stars: and **out of his mouth went a sharp twoedged sword:** and his countenance was as the sun shineth in his strength.
KJV

Rev 2:16
16 Repent; or else I will come unto thee quickly, and will **fight against them with the sword of my mouth.**
KJV

The flaming sword comes from God and is the two-edged sword of Christ's mouth. The Bible states that the Word of God is quick (living), and powerful, and sharper than any two-edged sword.

Heb 4:12-13
12 For **the word of God is quick, and powerful, and sharper than any twoedged sword,** piercing even to the dividing asunder of soul and spirit, and of the joints and marrow, and is a discerner of the thoughts and intents of the heart.
13 Neither is there any creature that is not manifest in his sight: but all things are naked and opened unto the eyes of him with whom we have to do.
KJV

Do you realize that every time you pick up the Bible, you are actually holding the sword that hides the way to the Garden and the tree of life? See there you go staring.

You have to realize that Christ is the Word of God, and the essence of Him is placed in the Bible that we read. The sword of the Spirit is the Word of God. The Bible shows us the way to the Garden of Eden, but it also keeps out those who seek to enter in without Christ. If you are in the Body of Christ, then studying the

Bible with the guidance of the Holy Spirit will lead you into the Holy of Holies to the mercy seat where we gain entrance to the Garden, which is a representation of God's Kingdom.

We learned earlier that the two angels that are on the mercy seat are the same two angels represented by the metaphor of the trees in the Garden. These two angels accompany the Lord of the whole earth. They are the two anointed ones that stand by the Lord of the whole earth. Satan's original position was one of the two angels. He was one of the cherubims, but was judged and replaced. The Lord of the whole earth is no other than Christ himself, who walked in the garden with Adam. He is the part of the Father sent to reveal all of the Father to men. Let me repeat this because it is very important. **He is the part of the Father sent to reveal all of the Father to men.** He is the flaming sword and the two cherubims stand next to him.

John 14:6
6 Jesus saith unto him, **I am the way**, the truth, and the life: no man cometh unto the Father, but by me.
KJV

The Greek word translated door actually means gate.

John 10:9
9 **I am the door**: by me if any man enter in, he shall be saved, and shall go in and out, and find pasture.
KJV

The Word of God will also allow you to see strong delusion if you try to enter in not being qualified by the blood of Jesus; you will find yourself way off track. This is why so many who study the Bible end up with doctrines that actually comes against the truth in God's Word, yet they believe they have truth:

2 Thess 2:10-12
10 And with all deceivableness of unrighteousness in them that perish; because they received not the love of the truth, that they might be saved.

11 And **for this cause God shall send them strong delusion, that they should believe a lie:**
12 That they all might be damned **who believed not the truth, but had pleasure in unrighteousness.**
KJV

I cannot count the amount of times I have spoken to unbelievers who don't believe the Bible but will be quick to quote it to support a false belief they hold. I have had those who believe that humankind has god potential like Hindus, five percent nation, Buddhist, and even atheist who believe humanity will evolve into gods quote Christ to support their false beliefs. They will say, "Even Christ said that we are gods," not understanding what Christ was saying yet they will believe without a shadow of a doubt that He was supporting what they believe. This is the scripture they are quoting:

John 10:34-36
34 **Jesus answered them, Is it not written in your law, I said, Ye are gods?**
35 **If he called them gods, unto whom the word of God came, and the scripture cannot be broken;**
36 Say ye of him, whom the Father hath sanctified, and sent into the world, Thou blasphemest; because I said, I am the Son of God?
KJV

Now if a person came to you and quoted this scripture would you believe you're a god? If you have the Holy Spirit, you will instantly know something is wrong. You will remember that trying to be like gods is what got Adam and Eve into a whole mess of trouble. You might not have the foundation to rightly divide the Word of God to realize that Christ was actually pointing out the ignorance of those who were questioning Him and in no way was He saying that humankind are gods. Yet if you do not have the truth in you (Spirit of Truth), then you will easily be swept up in the delusion and walk away believing you are some kind of god and the Bible confirms it.

Christ understood the real meaning of the scripture. He knew that the word gods used from the scripture He was quoting is elohim. He specifically said that they were called gods, "Unto whom the Word of God came." Christ knew that the Word of God came to

Israel and they were to be a nation of judges in the earth. The Hebrew word Elohim is translated judges as pertaining to Israel (EX 22:8). Israel was to bring judgment and righteousness to the world. Yet because of their wickedness and judging unrighteously that judgment would fall on their own heads. Christ was playing on the ignorance of the people who were rejecting Him and by which judgment would fall on them.

Ps 82
82:1 A Song or Psalm of A'-saph.
God standeth in the congregation of the mighty; he judgeth among the gods.
2 How long will ye judge unjustly, and accept the persons of the wicked? Selah.
3 Defend the poor and fatherless: do justice to the afflicted and needy.
4 Deliver the poor and needy: rid them out of the hand of the wicked.
5 They know not, neither will they understand; they walk on in darkness: all the foundations of the earth are out of course.
6 I have said, Ye are gods ; and all of you are children of the most High.
7 But ye shall die like men, and fall like one of the princes.
8 Arise, O God, judge the earth: for thou shalt inherit all nations.
KJV

There is a lot more in those verses but another place another time. I just want you to understand that the wicked can use the same verse that condemns them, to falsely support false doctrine that they believe. The Bible was written this way to keep the wicked out of the garden.

Yes, I know many pictured a garden sitting in some secret place hidden away on Earth that if you found your way there by wisdom or chance there would be a flaming sword blocking your path. You would then have to come up with magical words that would make the sword move aside and you would then enter the garden of Eden God's Paradise and have free access to the Tree of Life. Sorry to burst your bubble but I probably stopped you from wasting a whole lot of frequent flyer miles. (Smile)

Here is another misappropriated scripture being used to say people practicing other religions outside of Christianity and Judaism will be saved. The scripture below is speaking about the scattered Israelites and the gentiles coming to Christ to be saved. The unlearnt walking in ignorance has utilized it to support the delusion that you can worship other gods (and things), be a good person, and be saved.

John 10:16

16 And **other sheep I have, which are not of this fold**: them also I must bring, and they shall hear my voice; and there shall be one fold, and one shepherd.
KJV

I am shocked at the number of Christian pastors that are now entertaining the idea that there are other ways to heaven other than believing in Christ. Some have been as blasphemous as to say that good people of other religions with false gods such as Buddha, Khali, Allah, and pagan gods can make it in if they are good people. **None of us makes it in because we are good people; our righteousness is as filthy rags. Faith in Christ and His message of salvation is the only way in, and walking according to God's will is how we stay in.**

You can find life and the right pathway in the Bible but you can also get lost in your own delusions when you walk away from the truth. The Bible as the Word of God will facilitate any direction you're going in, thereby letting you in, or keeping you out. The sword of the Spirit is what guards the way to the Garden. The Pharisees studied the Bible religiously and were lost, using the very Bible to justify their delusions in rejecting Christ. Like many, they were forever learning yet unable to come to the knowledge of the truth: *We're dealing w/ Pharisees everyday.*

The Word of God was something that they studied yet when He, The Word of God, was standing before them they stumbled by rejecting the very gatekeeper to the Kingdom of God.

John 5:38-40

38 And ye have not his word abiding in you: for whom he hath sent, him ye believe not.

39 Search the scriptures; for in them ye think ye have eternal life: and they are they which testify of me.
40 And ye will not come to me, that ye might have life.
KJV

The sword lets you in and the sword keeps you out. This is how God hid Himself in plain view for everyone to find Him, according to His terms. This again confirms what I often say, **"When we meet God, it will be at His terms not ours."**

. Today you will be with me in Paradise

The mercy seat is the gate to the Garden of Eden; it is the entrance to paradise. This is why the high priest was required to put the blood at the east of the mercy seat, which represented the east where Adam and Eve were sent out of the Garden. This is why the cherubims and the flaming sword are set at the east of the Garden to guard the way to eternal life. I know this is a lot to take in, and many people reading this are saying; "Wow!" right now. Yet, Christ left us with one scene in the scriptures that confirms all of what I am saying.

Luke 23:38-43
38 And a superscription also was written over him in letters of Greek, and Latin, and Hebrew, THIS IS THE KING OF THE JEWS.
39 And one of the malefactors which were hanged railed on him, saying, If thou be Christ, save thyself and us.
40 But the other answering rebuked him, saying, Dost not thou fear God, seeing thou art in the same condemnation?
41 And we indeed justly; for we receive the due reward of our deeds: but this man hath done nothing amiss.
42 And he said unto Jesus, Lord, remember me when thou comest into thy kingdom.
43 And Jesus said unto him, Verily I say unto thee, **To day shalt thou be with me in paradise.**
KJV

Picture yourself standing on the hill of Golgotha. In front of you are three figures crucified. The imagery is burned into your mind as you zero in on Christ in the middle, and then the two other men to the right and to the left. One man is a good man that speaks life and the other man is an evil man that speaks death. The man in the middle is the Son of God, which is God in the flesh.

The scene changes, and now you are looking at two trees in the midst of the Garden with a bright light surrounded by a rainbow standing between them. One tree is a tree of life, and the other the tree of death that possesses the knowledge of good and evil. You realize that the thieves on the cross next to Christ are actually a representation of what you're now seeing.

The scene changes and you realize that the two trees are two cherubim angels of beautiful countenance, yet a shadow is over one because he has allowed his beauty and wisdom to corrupt him. He is to be judged and replaced.

The scene changes again, and you see two cherubim angels with a flaming sword in between them standing at the east of the Garden of Eden, and you realize it is to give entrance to or blockage against all who seek to enter the Paradise of God. It is the gate to the Garden the entrance to paradise.

The scene switches again, and you are standing in the Holy of Holies where you see two golden cherubims with their wings outspread and two of them touching covering the mercy seat where there is a glowing cloud of the glory of God. The front of the mercy seat, which is the side leading to the east, is covered by the blood of the Lamb, God's Salvation, Yehoshua, Jesus Christ of Nazareth. Suddenly you realize that you finally understand.

The vision brings you back to the three men being crucified and you again focus on the man in the middle with the pierced side with blood flowing out with water. You see the thorns on His head, the nails in his hands and heel. He is seconds away from death. You realize you know Him, not just recognize, but also really know Him. He is your Master, your Lord, your King, and your Savior. He is Emanuel God with us. He is the Light of the world, the Day Spring from on high, and the Bread of Life. He is king of Kings and Lord of Lords. Most importantly, He is your friend. He looks at you and smiles, and you realize that He knows you. He says seven words to you, **"You will be with me in Paradise!"**

Christ left me one last message for you:

Prov 8:22-36

22 The LORD possessed me in the beginning of his way, before his works of old.

23 I was set up from everlasting, from the beginning, or ever the earth was.

24 When there were no depths, I was brought forth; when there were no fountains abounding with water.

25 Before the mountains were settled, before the hills was I brought forth:

26 While as yet he had not made the earth, nor the fields, nor the highest part of the dust of the world.

27 When he prepared the heavens, I was there: when he set a compass upon the face of the depth:

28 When he established the clouds above: when he strengthened the fountains of the deep:

29 When he gave to the sea his decree, that the waters should not pass his commandment: when he appointed the foundations of the earth:

30 Then I was by him, as one brought up with him: and I was daily his delight, rejoicing always before him;

31 Rejoicing in the habitable part of his earth; and my delights were with the sons of men.

32 Now therefore hearken unto me, O ye children: for blessed are they that keep my ways.

33 Hear instruction, and be wise, and refuse it not.

34 Blessed is the man that heareth me, watching daily at my gates, waiting at the posts of my doors.

35 For whoso findeth me findeth life, and shall obtain favour of the LORD.

36 But he that sinneth against me wrongeth his own soul: all they that hate me love death.

KJV

Be Blessed!

The Need for Salvation

If you are reading (or have read) this book and you do not know Christ Jesus as your personal Savior, all it takes is a simple prayer to change your circumstance and start you on the pathway to eternal life. Christ came and died in your place to save you from sin and eternal damnation. Do you understand why His death was necessary? God did not create the world to be wicked and to perish, but He did give all humanity freewill. When Adam sinned in disobeying God, it allowed wickedness to enter the world through sin. God has appointed a day to judge the wickedness of this world.

God loves the creation He has made. He sent his Son Jesus (Yehoshua) to redeem the earth and all those who believe (accept Christ and walk in His truth) that God sent His Son to die so that we all might live.

Christ's death and resurrection from the dead enables us to come back into relationship with the Father. He took the penalty of death for us to remove our sins, and bring us back into a right relationship with God. With a right relationship comes the renewal of our spirit, which allows us to sense and understand spiritual things. His resurrection represents our spiritual renewing and the hope of eternal life in God's Kingdom.

(Precious Bible Promises)

YOU ARE A SINNER…
Rom 3:10
10 As it is written, There is none righteous, no, not one:

1 John 1:8
8 If we say that we have no sin, we deceive ourselves, and the truth is not in us.

Rom 3:23
23 For all have sinned, and come short of the glory of God;

THERE IS A PRICE TO BE PAID FOR SIN...
Eph 5:3-7
3 But fornication, and all uncleanness, or covetousness, let it not be once named among you, as becometh saints;
4 Neither filthiness, nor foolish talking, nor jesting, which are not convenient: but rather giving of thanks.
5 For this ye know, that no whoremonger, nor unclean person, nor covetous man, who is an idolater, hath any inheritance in the kingdom of Christ and of God.
6 Let no man deceive you with vain words: for because of these things cometh the wrath of God upon the children of disobedience.
7 Be not ye therefore partakers with them.

Gal 5:19-21
19 Now the works of the flesh are manifest, which are these; Adultery, fornication, uncleanness, lasciviousness,
20 Idolatry, witchcraft, hatred, variance, emulations, wrath, strife, seditions, heresies,
21 Envyings, murders, drunkenness, revellings, and such like: of the which I tell you before, as I have also told you in time past, that they which do such things shall not inherit the kingdom of God.

1 Cor 6:9-10
9 Know ye not that the unrighteous shall not inherit the kingdom of God? Be not deceived: neither fornicators, nor idolaters, nor adulterers, nor effeminate, nor abusers of themselves with mankind,
10 Nor thieves, nor covetous, nor drunkards, nor revilers, nor extortioners, shall inherit the kingdom of God.

GOD TAKES NO PLEASURE IN ANYONE GOING TO HELL...
Ezek 33:11
11 Say unto them, As I live, saith the Lord GOD, I have no pleasure in the death of the wicked; but that the wicked turn from his way and live: turn ye, turn ye from your evil ways; for why will ye die, O house of Israel?

1 Tim 2:4
4 Who will have all men to be saved, and to come unto the knowledge of the truth.

NEED OF REPENTANCE...
2 Peter 3:9

9 The Lord is not slack concerning his promise, as some men count slackness; but is longsuffering to us-ward, not willing that any should perish, but that all should come to repentance.

Luke 5:32

32 I came not to call the righteous, but sinners to repentance.

Acts 3:19

19 Repent ye therefore, and be converted, that your sins may be blotted out, when the times of refreshing shall come from the presence of the Lord;

GOD LOVES YOU...
Rev 3:19-20

19 As many as I love, I rebuke and chasten: be zealous therefore, and repent.
20 Behold, I stand at the door, and knock: if any man hear my voice, and open the door, I will come in to him, and will sup with him, and he with me.

GOD SENT HIS SON JESUS TO SAVE YOU...
Matt 18:11

11 For the Son of man is come to save that which was lost.

John 3:16-18

16 For God so loved the world, that he gave his only begotten Son, that whosoever believeth in him should not perish, but have everlasting life.
17 For God sent not his Son into the world to condemn the world; but that the world through him might be saved.
18 He that believeth on him is not condemned: but he that believeth not is condemned already, because he hath not believed in the name of the only begotten Son of God.

CHRIST DIED FOR YOU AND WANTS TO SAVE YOU...
Rom 6:23

23 For the wages of sin is death; but the gift of God is eternal life through Jesus Christ our Lord.

Rom 5:6-8

6 For when we were yet without strength, in due time Christ died for the ungodly.

7 For scarcely for a righteous man will one die: yet peradventure for a good man some would even dare to die.

8 But God commendeth his love toward us, in that, while we were yet sinners, Christ died for us.

CHRIST CAN SAVE YOU NOW...

Rom 10:9-10

9 That if thou shalt confess with thy mouth the Lord Jesus, and shalt believe in thine heart that God hath raised him from the dead, thou shalt be saved.

10 For with the heart man believeth unto righteousness; and with the mouth confession is made unto salvation.

YOU CAN KNOW THAT YOU'RE SAVED...

1 John 5:10-13

10 He that believeth on the Son of God hath the witness in himself: he that believeth not God hath made him a liar; because he believeth not the record that God gave of his Son.

11 And this is the record, that God hath given to us eternal life, and this life is in his Son.

12 He that hath the Son hath life; and he that hath not the Son of God hath not life.

13 These things have I written unto you that believe on the name of the Son of God; that ye may know that ye have eternal life, and that ye may believe on the name of the Son of God.

A Sinner's Prayer...

Father, the Creator of all things, I come to You today and confess that I am a sinner. I confess that I believe that You sent your Son Christ Jesus to die for my sins to bring me back into relationship with You. I accept what He has done and repent for all my past sins. (Confess all pass sins that you can remember.) Forgive me Father, renew my spirit, and lead me in the way of righteousness. I ask this in the name of your Son Jesus Christ. AMEN!

Maranatha!

References

Fausset's Bible Dictionary, Electronic Database Copyright (c)1998, 2003 by Biblesoft

International Standard Bible Encyclopaedia, Electronic Database Copyright © 1996, 2003 by Biblesoft, Inc. All rights reserved.)

Precious Bible Promises (From the New King James Version) (c) 1983 Thomas Nelson, Publishers.

Williams Samuel, The Truth about the Tithe Copyright (c) 2016

Williams Samuel, Assault on Innocence Copyright (c) 2017

NOTE FROM THE AUTHOR:

I just wanted to take a moment to thank you for taking this journey with me. If this book was a blessing to you please let me know at Samuelkem@aol.com, or visit the book's Facebook page "Hidden in the Garden" and like. I will personally respond to each email and answer questions asked. I will also share with you information on upcoming books and revelations. Please feel free to ask questions or post comments on the Facebook page also. Be blessed.

☆ be on guard
☆ Stay alert
☆ be watchful

devour - to destroy, to ruin The Soul, to slay, to eat up
Satan seeks to devour us.

Made in the USA
Lexington, KY
11 April 2019